THE FINCHER FILE

THE FINCHER FILE

Terry Fincher and Tony Lynch

QUARTET BOOKS

LONDON MELBOURNE NEW YORK

First published by Quartet Books Limited, 1981
A member of the Namara Group
27/29 Goodge Street, London W1P IFD

ISBN 0 7043 2293 5

British Library Cataloguing in Publication Data
Fincher, Terry
  The Fincher File.
  1. Fincher, Terry
  2. Photographers – England – Biography
  I. Title   II. Lynch, Tony
  770'.92'4   TR140.F/

Typeset by Amicon Print Ltd, Wallington, Surrey
Printed in Great Britain by Hazell, Watson & Viney Ltd,
Aylesbury, Bucks

For June

Contents

Acknowledgements

The authors would like to thank the following individuals for their help in the preparation of this book: Alan Barlow, David Daye, Jayne Fincher, June Fincher, Pauline Longbon, Pam Lynch, John Melhuish and Hugh Wills.

Also the following organizations for permission to reproduce photographs: Express Group Newspapers, Keystone Press, Mirror Group Newspapers, the *Sun* newspaper, Syndication International.

Foreword

During the course of research for this book I visited Terry Fincher's home village, Oving, in Buckinghamshire. There I met a man named Mr Midwinter, who proudly proclaimed that he was 86 and Oving's oldest inhabitant. I asked him where the Fincher family had lived and he took me to a small cottage opposite a recreation ground. He spoke of Fincher's father for a while, then I asked him what he knew of the son, Terry.

'There was a very strong rumour going about once, that he won some important award in the photography business,' replied Mr Midwinter.

In fact, Terry Fincher is one of the world's leading photo-journalists and has won the top award in British Press photography – The Press Photographer of the Year Award – four times (a record). His work is internationally respected and appears consistently in newspapers and magazines all over the globe.

His career began in 1945 when he joined Keystone, the famous Fleet Street picture agency, as a messenger-boy. Since then he has worked on the staff of three national dailies, the *Daily Herald*, the *Daily Express* and the *Sun*. In 1969 he left Fleet Street to go freelance and eventually formed his own agency, Photographers International, which today syndicates his own work world-wide.

Terry is always totally involved in his current assignment whatever it may be. He is an enthusiastic, energetic and emotional man – qualities which are ultimately reflected in his photography. This is his story, and I hope it gives some substance to that innocently understated 'rumour' first reported to me by Mr Midwinter.

Tony Lynch
July 1981

1

Suez 1956 – The Turning Point

The turning point in my career came when I was least expecting it – on a blustery October evening in 1956. I was 25 years old and working for Keystone Press, the well-known Fleet Street picture agency. I had been a full-time professional with the agency since my demobilization from the army in 1951 and, although not particularly well paid, I regarded myself as a reasonably successful photographer. I had covered many important stories around Britain, and in 1954 I had been on my first foreign assignment – to photograph Field-Marshal Montgomery unveiling the Alamein Memorial in Egypt; I had been to Baghdad to cover the British Trade Fair there; and had recently photographed the opening of the Windscale atomic power station, by the Queen, and the official visit to London by the Russian leaders, Bulganin and Khrushchev. My work was being published regularly in the national newspapers. Yet, with the inner drive common to all ambitious people, I was feeling very restless. At times it seemed the world was passing me by. In truth, I was itching to get stuck into a story with a bit more action.

That evening – Monday 29 October – I arrived at my flat in Sydenham, south-east London, and settled down with my young wife June in front of the TV, to watch the ITN news bulletin. The newsreader appeared on the screen and within seconds he gravely announced that Israel had launched a military attack on Egypt.

Trouble had been brewing in Egypt since the withdrawal, in July, of British and American funds which were to have financed the building of a dam at Aswan on the Upper Nile. Following the withdrawal Colonel Nasser had seized control of the Suez Canal, and to recoup his losses planned to charge dues on all shipping using the canal. As a third of this shipping was British and almost a quarter of British imports arrived via the canal, it had come as no surprise when Prime Minister Anthony Eden dramatically declared: 'The Egyptian has his thumb on our windpipe!' It now seemed likely that a combined Israeli-Franco-British attack on the Canal Zone would soon take place, to settle the matter once and for all.

June turned to me and said: 'That's the sort of story you'd like to cover isn't it?' She was right, of course, I felt great envy for those of my Fleet Street colleagues who would be flying out to cover the crisis – it was exactly the sort of story I wanted to get my teeth into.

As I sat there brooding, I heard the door-bell ring. June went downstairs to answer it and came back with Fred, the Keystone driver. He gave a typewritten note while June poured him a cup of tea. (We had no telephone, and messages from Midge Aylward, my Editor, would often arrive by hand.)

'Must be important, Terry,' said Fred. 'I was just going home when they gave it to me. They said I was to get it to you right away.'

I read the note:

FINCHER . . . YOU WILL BE LEAVING TOMORROW AFTERNOON FOR DESTINATION UNKNOWN . . . BUT YOU CAN GUESS TO WHAT PART OF THE WORLD . . . YOU ARE BEING ACCREDITED TO THE BRITISH FORCES AND NOT UNDER YOUR OWN STEAM TO TEL AVIV . . . WHERE YOU WILL BE LANDED I DO NOT KNOW BUT TAKE-OFF BY AIR IS 2.30 PM TOMORROW. MAKE SURE YOU BRING IN TOMORROW ALL NECESSARY CLOTHING, PASSPORT, VACCINATION PAPERS ETC. THAT YOU MAY WANT . . . YOU CAN RING ME AT HOME THIS EVENING FOR FURTHER DETAILS . . .

I passed the note to June. She read it twice, then glanced at the TV set. 'Suez?' she asked quietly. 'Will it be dangerous?'

'Rather you than me, mate,' said Fred between sips.

A pained expression crossed June's face, and Fred saw that it was time for him to leave: 'Thanks for the cuppa, June,' he said awkwardly. 'And good luck, Terry.' I thanked him and saw him out.

It was the beginning of a tearful evening for June and me; we were about to be parted for the first time in just over a year of marriage. We sat down to our evening meal, but neither of us had much of an appetite. Later,

I began to get ready for the journey ahead and realized – now that my 'big moment' had actually arrived – how hopelessly unprepared I was. I had no cash in my pocket, so I borrowed £3 from June – all that was left of the week's housekeeping money. 'Bring . . . all necessary clothing . . .', the message had read, but I had little clothing to bring, certainly nothing suitable for the heat of the Middle East. I simply packed the lightest things I could find and hoped for the best. I checked my cameras, a 2¼ square Rolleiflex and an MPP 5 × 4, and carefully put them inside my camera-case along with my passport and vaccination certificates. And that was it; I was ready for action. But, in the sad silence that followed the packing, my great ambition seemed somehow stupid and unnecessary.

Next morning I was up even earlier than usual. I kissed June good-bye and was gone before her tears could begin again. I made my way to the Keystone offices, in Red Lion Court, off Fleet Street, to receive last-minute instructions from Midge and collect traveller's cheques and extra film stock. Several members of the staff wished me luck, and the General Manager, George Pratt, called me into his office. George had been a kind of father figure to me since my early days with the agency and had always encouraged me in my photography.

'Well, boy, this is your big chance,' he said. 'Have you got your money?'

I told him I had £3 of my own and that I had drawn £40 from the accounts department – a sizeable sum in those days.

'Well, keep in touch, look after yourself and remember: this is a major assignment. We're counting on you,' he said as we shook hands

I felt very proud of myself at that moment, but as I walked along windy Fleet Street once more I was already missing June and our cosy flat, and this feeling turned quickly to loneliness. However, I knew there was no turning back and my spirits had lifted again by the time I reached the War Office, in Whitehall, where together with several other photographers and journalists I was officially sworn in as a war correspondent. Next stop was London airport.

The Heathrow of 1956 was a far cry from the sophisticated airport we know today. Commercial air travel was barely out of its infancy and prop-aircraft were the order of the day. The spluttering of an aircraft engine coming to life would occasionally drift across the tarmac, and every so often a plane would thunder along against a backdrop of several large grey hangars, before lifting itself into the air. The Arrivals and Departures area consisted of little more than a few prefabricated huts on the north side of the airport. Tucked away in the corner was a tea and coffee counter, with steam rising from its urns, where a few travellers stood sipping from thick white cups; others stood outside, with collars turned up against the wind, as they said good-bye to their loved ones. It was a sad scene which matched my feelings perfectly.

I spied a newspaper kiosk. The placards read: BOMBERS ATTACK EGYPT. I bought a paper and read of Israel's attack advancing towards Suez: it sent a shiver of excitement through me.

Time was ticking away fast and I had promised to call June at her office before leaving. Eventually I found what seemed to be the only telephone kiosk in the airport. It was occupied by a very large woman who must have sensed my anxiety but showed no sign of ever coming out. She was still talking into the phone when my flight was announced over the Tannoy, so I left without making the call.

The War Office had chartered a plane to take our Press party to the Middle East. They hadn't told us where exactly we were headed – it was still 'destination unknown' – but we knew there would be a brief stop for refuelling in Naples.

Anyone observing our departure could easily have mistaken our jovial bunch for a party of rugby supporters; in no way did we give the appearance of men going off to war. I was as cheerful as the rest, but as London and the English countryside disappeared beneath a layer of cloud I grew depressed once more. At that moment I genuinely believed I would never see June again and, over-dramatic though it sounds, I believed I was on my way to witness the end of the world.

There were drinks on board, as there usually are at any gathering of journalists. I had one stiff Scotch, then another. By my third drink I had decided to enjoy the experiences that lay ahead. I took comfort in the company of two of my colleagues: Horace Tonge, a fellow-photographer and an old friend of mine, who was laughing and joking in his broad North-country accent, and Cyril Page, an ITN cameraman who looked supremely cool and confident in his ultra-smart suit as he recalled his adventures in the Korean war. These were men who had been to war before. They had always come home, I reasoned, so why shouldn't I? I had another Scotch, then fell asleep. Someone woke me up as we were about to land at Naples, and informed me that our 'destination unknown' had at last been revealed – we were heading for Cyprus.

An electrical storm made it impossible to take off again on the second leg of our journey, to Nicosia, so I joined three of my new friends on a tour of Naples. Naturally this involved visiting several bars. Next morning I woke up in my hotel room, nursing a terrific hangover, a condition hardly improved by thoughts of the flight ahead. My companions of the night before seemed none the worse for our tour of the city and continuously teased me with impersonations of an Italian female calling: 'Hey, bigga boy – you wanna pussy?' I had no idea what they were talking about.

The flight to Nicosia was very rough as we flew through the bad weather we had avoided the night before. At one point the plane passed through an air-pocket and everyone was thrown to the ceiling of the cabin. Luckily there was only one casualty, a stewardess who unfortunately gashed her head. As far as I was concerned, the only good thing about the flight was that it cleared mine.

We were met at Nicosia airport by a smart, good-looking young officer who introduced himself as Captain Michael Parkinson – later to become famous as a TV chat-show presenter. He was part of 4PRS – the Army Press unit – and was one of the conducting officers whose duty it was to look after visiting journalists. His first task was to transport us to the Ledra Palace Hotel and book us in for the night. The fragrance of cedar trees saturated the early evening air as we drove through the streets of the city. This was my first impression of Cyprus and one I always recall with fondness.

At the hotel I found myself sharing a room with the ever-jolly Horace Tonge. We were both completely shattered after our long journey and gratefully crashed out on our beds. I had just begun to drift into a welcome sleep when Mike Parkinson came in.

'You've to get to a briefing – right away,' he announced, full of bright-eyed enthusiasm. For a moment I thought I was back in the bloody army! I struggled up off the bed and into my shoes, then followed Mike and Horace out of the hotel and onto a bus filled with my yawning travelling companions of the past two days.

Mike took us to the nerve centre of the Anglo-French operation, a large briefing room, its walls covered with maps of the Middle East. He introduced us to the commanders of the operation, Generals Stockwell and Darling, who both stood before a huge table on which were spread even more maps.

We were told that the invasion fleet was assembling elsewhere in the Mediterranean and that the combined attack was imminent. A small volunteer Press party was invited to go in with the first assault, to cover the event – on a pool basis – for the world's media. My enthusiasm immediately overcame my exhaustion and my hand shot into the air before anyone else had a chance.

Among others who volunteered for this first rota group were: Cyril Page, Hanson Baldwin of the *New York Times*, Seaghan Maynes of Reuters and Donald Edgar, a reporter on the *Daily Express*.

As we were to leave that night, Captain Parkinson had hastily arranged for all the pool party to be kitted out in army uniforms at the QM stores. I was supplied with a

baggy tunic and trousers to match, made of rough, heavy material, the usual Army issue; nothing could have been more unsuitable for wearing in the Mediterranean climate, not even the typically English clothes I had packed for the journey. The trousers stayed up only with difficulty and I looked awkward, to say the least. But I didn't care; I had official 'War Correspondent' flashes on my shoulders and with the honorary rank of Captain I was feeling very proud of myself, especially as I hadn't risen above Private in my National Service days.

There was just enough time for me to return to the hotel to collect my unpacked suitcase and cameras and eat a quick meal. I said good-bye to Horace, then made my way down to the lobby where some very attractive air-stewardesses were booking in for the night. They glanced disbelievingly at me as I shuffled across the floor carrying my luggage in one hand and holding up my trousers with the other. Savas, the night-porter, who was later to become a good friend of mine, watched me with his permanently sad eyes, knowing he stood no chance of a tip. I glanced up at the clock above his desk. It was midnight.

In 1956 Cyprus was in the throes of civil unrest – Grivas and EOKA were conducting a terrorist campaign against British rule on the island – each day brought fresh reports of a bombing or shooting incident, and it was considered unsafe and foolish to travel anywhere at night. However, under Captain Parkinson's command, our small group of volunteer pressmen sped off into the darkness in a hired taxi, heading for the port of Famagusta where we were to board a troop-ship which would take us to Egypt. Our driver was not happy. He couldn't see the sense in being a prime target for the terrorists, but the promise of a doubled fare was enough to spur him on in the face of adversity. His nervousness transmitted itself to me, and my confidence wilted somewhat when Mike laughingly informed us that he had forgotten to take his revolver out of his kit-bag, which was in the boot of the taxi. So we drove on, unarmed, eventually arriving in Famagusta in the still hours of morning, only to be informed by the Duty Officer at the dock gates that we should have gone to Limassol, some fifty miles to the west. Our gallant Captain had been given the wrong orders!

The unfortunate taxi-driver was in a state of near-collapse by the time we arrived in Limassol, where we booked into a small hotel just as the orange dawn was lighting the streets.

Two hours later I was awakened with the news that we were about to board the *Empire Ken* – an ex-Irish Channel ferry converted into a troop-ship – for the last leg of our journey. Before leaving the hotel we were able to enjoy a delicious breakfast of bacon and eggs, a tasty reminder of home. The proprietor's English wife took pity on me and altered my uniform, ensuring that my trousers would stay up on their own and taking at least six inches off each leg into the bargain!

The *Empire Ken* was anchored half a mile

off-shore and as we chugged towards her, in a small, overcrowded boat, we could see the decks littered with British troops resting in the sun. On board, our Press-gang was put into a small relatively private cabin. The heat was uncomfortable and it was a relief to find a bar on the top deck where I bought a refreshing shandy – not available to other ranks. 'Christ! It really is "them and us"!' I thought, recalling my own days as an 'other rank'. But, by then, I was too tired to care. I just wanted to take off my itchy 'uniform' and get my head down for some proper sleep. After all, I would need all the energy I could muster for we would be seeing action in a matter of hours – or so I thought.

Two days later the *Ken* was still cruising around the Mediterranean. The official reason given for the delay was that we were waiting for the fleet to assemble. Among the troops it was generally believed that those in charge hadn't a clue what they were doing. In fact, as we later learned, the blame lay in

Royal Navy helicopter evacuating wounded near Casino Palace Hotel, Port Said

a series of compromises between the politicians in Washington, Paris and London.

Our only contact with the rest of the world was the BBC Overseas News on the radio, heralded by its familiar signature tune 'Lillibullero'. On 5 November the newsreader informed us that a large Anglo-French Fleet was heading across the Mediterranean towards Suez; and John Foster Dulles, the then US Secretary of State, had ordered the US 6th Fleet to cruise alongside. Meanwhile, in Hungary, Russian troops were entering Budapest, street-fighting was taking place there and many people had been killed.

Next morning, 6 November, the *Empire Ken* began to move southwards towards Port Said, and on either side of the ship we could see the fleet moving slowly forward through the blue sea. Later on we could see the outline of land in the distance, and an air of anticipation shrouded the ship as the troops prepared themselves for the landing. An hour or so later, clouds of smoke could be seen rising on the horizon and several French *Mystère* jet-fighters were diving at targets at the entrance to the Suez Canal.

We were told that we would soon be going ashore. I went below to check my cameras and slides. I saw myself reflected in the cabin mirror as another *Mystère* flew overhead, I thought, 'What the bloody hell are you doing here?' Then someone called out, 'Come up on deck, we're going in soon.'

We were transferred to a large landing-barge for the last 100 yards and I could hear the cracking sound of gunfire as we moved in. More *Mystères* screamed low overhead. I was scared and my hands were sweating as I clutched my camera-case. I looked around at my companions in the craft: soldiers were sitting nervously quiet, lost in their own thoughts; only their sergeant seemed able to hide his feelings completely. Cyril Page was his usual cool, calm self and looked every inch the self-assured professional in his Canadian Army uniform. Captain Parkinson was with us and I wondered if he was as nervous as me – at least he wore a brave smile on his face.

The barge bumped up against the quay-side and the sounds of shooting, jet-fighters and helicopters all merged into one. I slipped as I jumped ashore, badly gashing my leg on the side of the barge. My camera-case dropped into the water, and I quickly pulled it out again, hoping that nothing inside was damaged. Other landing craft were off-loading, and soldiers were heading in the direction of the Casino Palace Hotel. I saw Cyril Page heading in that direction, too, and I decided to follow him. 'It's like D-Day all over again,' he said casually as another *Mystère* screamed overhead to launch yet another attack on the Canal Company offices.

I began taking pictures as we ran and almost tripped over the body of a British soldier covered by a blanket. Then I paused to photograph the evacuation of wounded soldiers by a Royal Navy helicopter. I saw other injured soldiers, British and Egyptian, being carried into the hotel to receive treatment on the tables in the billiard room – once used by passengers travelling in the great ships to the Far East. I looked around. Cyril was gone.

I ran along the sea-front and saw some wooden beach-huts in the distance. They were built on stilts, with straw roofing laid loosely on top; I ran towards them. Suddenly bullets whistled past my head. 'Jesus! They're shooting at me!' I thought, running even faster towards the huts, with the camera-case banging heavily against my leg and sweat pouring off me. I dived headlong beneath one of the huts and lay breathless in the sand, trying to collect my thoughts. I had just begun to change the film in my slides when the hut above me erupted in a vivid sheet of flame and noise. I scrambled clear, dragging my camera-case with me, then began to run again, away from the danger. I was covered in dust; it was in my eyes and in my mouth. I ran into Cyril Page; he told me an ammunition truck had been hit, sending the bullets flying everywhere. He took me to a car which he'd 'liberated' from somewhere and drove further along the front to a new area of action.

Egyptian mother chasing the cart which carries the body of her dead son

Perhaps the most poignant picture I took that day is of a black-shawled Egyptian mother chasing the cart which carried the body of her dead son; they were taking him off for burial. I managed to stop the cart and she was able to spend a few moments cradling her son's body in a final farewell.

The Egyptians surrendered within 12 hours. Port Said was under British control once more and a cease-fire was called.

Thanks to Mike Parkinson, who told me that nearby El Gamel airfield had been captured by British paratroopers, I was able to get my films on board a small plane about to take off for Cyprus, where they would be transferred to a Canberra jet headed for London.

Meanwhile, the *Empire Ken* had tied up at the quayside. Back on board I patched up my leg and took a much needed shower, trying to wash the dirt and smell of battle from my skin. I was shattered after my first day as a war photographer, but nothing could dispel the euphoria I felt. I knew I had done a good job and hoped my films would reach London safely. In fact, they arrived in Fleet Street well ahead of any other correspondent's copy or film. The momentary dip in the sea had not damaged my cameras and my pictures were published during the following days in newspapers all over the world. (Later, I learned that a British newspaperman had reached Suez some 12 hours ahead of our arrival on the *Ken*. He was Peter Woods of the *Daily Mirror*, later to become well-known as a BBC-TV newscaster. He had somehow conned his way on board an RAF plane and had jumped at dawn with the 'paras'. Unfortunately Peter fractured his ankle on landing and he had to withdraw.)

Next day, several other correspondents arrived and a Press HQ was set up in a block of flats 'air-conditioned' by shell holes. We were reasonably comfortable there until the sewage system broke down, making the place uninhabitable. We transferred to HMS *Forth*, an old naval submarine depot-ship from Malta, serving as the task force communications HQ.

During the early days of Suez, communications between correspondents and their respective offices were chaotic, to say the least. I received a cable from George Pratt, bawling me out for not keeping in touch, while at the same time informing me of the great success of my first pictures.

While on board HMS *Forth* I teamed up with an old friend, Larry Burrows, a *Life* magazine photographer. Larry seemed familiar with practically every piece of photographic equipment ever manufactured. He was forever talking about cameras and was using 35-mm Leicas for his coverage of the crisis. I had to admit that they were lightweight and easy to use compared to my equipment, but like most other Fleet Street photographers it would be at least two years before I put my trust in 'miniature' cameras, thereby lightening my load considerably.

The Suez troubles were contained within a small area running alongside the canal, so it was reasonably easy to reach a trouble-spot very quickly. In the first week Larry and I drove to El Gamel. On the way we stopped to talk to a bomb-disposal officer and watched from a safe distance as he defused two land-mines. On our return to base we learned that he had been killed while attempting to defuse a third mine. Another day we came across the sickening sight of a pile of dead Egyptian soldiers lying bloated and stinking in the heat.

Three days after the cease-fire David Seymour of Magnum and Jean Roy of *Paris Match* were driving along a stretch of road in 'No-man's-land' between the Suez and Sweetwater canals when a young Egyptian guard panicked and opened fire on them. Their jeep left the road and fell into the Sweetwater canal. They were the first photographers of my acquaintance to be killed in action.

It was a great relief when it became my turn to fly back to Nicosia to replenish the Press HQ's stocks of food and drink. I was to stay overnight in the Ledra Palace Hotel and looked forward to sleeping between clean sheets again.

It was in the Ledra Palace bar that I first met Derek Lambert, a young reporter from the *Daily Mirror*, now a well-known author. He was tall, good-looking and smartly dressed, with a sense of style which really impressed me. He also had a newspaper expense account which impressed me even more (national newspapers could always afford to be more generous than the agencies). Derek invited me to join him for dinner that evening, along with two very pretty air-stewardesses. I told him I'd like to accept but explained that I had no clothes suitable for such an occasion. He offered to lend me a jacket for the evening. Our friendship, which has lasted ever since, was cemented with a howl of laughter from Derek when I entered the restaurant with the tails of his enormous jacket flapping somewhere around my thighs. However,

despite its funny start, the evening was not a success; I was feeling homesick and could think only of June and of the day when I'd get back to her.

That day came sooner than I expected for I was recalled to London a week before Christmas.

I knew I had fared well on my first major assignment, but I was genuinely surprised by the warm reception I got back in Fleet Street. Keystone were more than happy with my success and I was promised other valuable assignments in the New Year. My reunion with June was a joyful one and we spent a marvellous Christmas together.

In Britain the whole Suez episode was looked upon as a gigantic folly and what had begun as 'Eden's War' eventually led to the same Prime Minister's resignation. He was succeeded by Harold Macmillan. Although the combined assault had resulted in an overwhelming military victory, the moral victory went to Egypt. Following the British

Commandos raise the White Ensign over Navy House, ten minutes after capturing the building

Captain Michael Parkinson (left) and I near the front-line

withdrawal, Nasser was able to complete his Aswan dam project with a freshly negotiated loan.

Keystone were true to their word and I found myself assigned to more and more important stories. My photography improved greatly and I entered a portfolio in the 1957 British Press Photographer of the Year Competition, organized by the publishers of *Encyclopaedia Britannica* and the Institute of British Photographers.

One day, in the winter, I was on a routine assignment outside the Russian Embassy, waiting to photograph a high-ranking official of the KGB – his visit to London was the cause of much controversy – when Charlie Dawson, a photographer from Planet News, tapped me on the shoulder and told me that I had won the Press Photographer of the Year Award.

For once I was stunned into silence; this was the highest award in the game and I had considered my chances of winning it to be very remote indeed. For the next few days I wandered around in a daze as people, some of them highly respected in Fleet Street, congratulated me.

I was presented with the Hector McNeill Trophy and a cheque for 100 guineas, by Lord Montgomery of Alamein, at the Savoy Hotel on 19 December. I was the youngest photographer ever to win the award.

2

Beginnings

My father Len Fincher had been a promising athlete in his youth and a runner of potential international standard (he once confided with no small pride that he had run the mile in just over four minutes on the Iffley Road track in Oxford). In 1923 he was at the top of his form and had high hopes of being selected for the national team. Instead, he caught pneumonia and his athletics career came to an abrupt end.

While recovering in Stoke Mandeville hospital he was tended by a young Irish nurse named Ruth Walker. Their relationship soon developed beyond usual nurse/patient limits and before leaving the hospital he proposed marriage to her. That winter they rode his motorcycle through a snowstorm to High Wycombe where, in the best romantic tradition, they were married in secret. They settled in a small cottage in the village of Oving, seven miles to the north of Aylesbury in Buckinghamshire.

Len was a native of the village and something of a local character. He was an extrovert who more than liked his pint and the bright lights of Aylesbury. By contrast, Ruth was a shy and gentle woman. These differences in their personalities which had perhaps not been so apparent in the hospital

ward later caused much tension between them.

My brother Mike was born in 1927. I made my entry into the world four years later (on 8 July 1931) at the Royal Bucks hospital in Aylesbury. According to my father I was born during a thunderstorm – bright flashes of light and very loud bangs have certainly played a prominent part in my life ever since!

The Great Depression gripped most of the country during my infancy. My father, like many other young men of his time, took to drinking too much and in order to pay for his pint and the privilege of drowning his sorrows he began pawning his hard-won athletics cups and medals, a habit which earned him the nickname 'Hocking' among his friends. My mother, like the rest of the Walker family, was thrifty by nature and she found it difficult to accept such extravagance, thereby adding to the troubles between her and my father. Consequently Mike and I spent much of our childhood beneath the clouds of our parents' constant bickering.

Often, whenever it seemed likely that a new row was about to erupt, we would head for our grandparents' house just a few

My father, Len Fincher

hundred yards away, where a warm welcome always awaited us. Our grandparents were, of course, well aware of the troubles at home. They knew what Len, the youngest of their three sons – the proverbial 'black sheep' of the family – was like but they never interfered in his marriage, hoping that everything would right itself in the end.

They were strict Methodists. Grandad was a part-time preacher who travelled the village chapel circuit most Sundays. He never touched alcohol, but he did enjoy a pipe filled with sweet-smelling tobacco. Grandma, on the other hand, did like the occasional glass of Guinness and would often ask me to smuggle a bottle or two past Grandad when she sent me to the shop for lemonade.

Thankfully, this wise old couple exerted a stabilizing effect on our young lives, making it seem that things were perhaps not so bad at home, after all, especially for us two brothers.

Mike became my hero. He was four years my senior and seemed so clever compared to me. He always did well at school and never failed to do the right thing, while I was forever in some kind of trouble. I began to follow him around hoping to discover the secret of his success. I became his shadow, completely oblivious to the fact that he hated my constant attention. One day, unable to bear the frustration any longer, he shoved me down a drain, replaced the iron grating and left me there. Luckily my cries for help were heard by a passing woman who, with the help of her husband, lifted the grating and hauled me out. Mike got a belting from Dad that night, but probably considered it worth while as I never followed him quite so devotedly again.

Around this time my father was running a one-man window-cleaning and firewood business among the surrounding villages. His transport was an ordinary bicycle with a third wheel attached to support the wooden platform that carried his wares. I often accompanied him on his rounds, and would sit among the bundles of firewood on the platform as he rode from village to village. It took all day and several journeys to sell all the bundles and we'd return home at dusk, invariably stopping at the Swan, a pub in Whitchurch. I used to sit outside minding the bike and sniffing the pleasant beery smell that came from the bar until eventually my father would emerge again, fully refreshed. Then, a little groggily, he would pedal the remaining mile to Oving, guided only by the light of an oil lamp clamped to the side of the bike. The lamp's weak beam was unable to penetrate very far into the darkness and I'd sit nervously in the gloom, listening to my father's breathing and the squeak of the bike. Being an imaginative child I was certain we would collide with some terrible monster of the night lurking in the dark.

I have many memories of those distant days: of the seasons coming and going, displaying a far greater contrast than they do today; of summers that were long and hot and lazy; of the roadworkers arriving with their scythes to cut down the long grass and nettles on the verges. I remember when, at midday, we would sit with the workmen and share some of the cold tea they always carried in enamel jugs or lemonade bottles.

At the front in the baggy pants, with my mother and Michael. The picture was taken in Oving on washday by a travelling photographer

Autumn brought streets full of fallen leaves and the sound of rooks cawing in the bare trees across the fields. In winter it always snowed and the village was sometimes cut off from the rest of the world by huge snow-drifts. We would toboggan for hours on home-made wooden sleds down Oving Hill then return home, with chapped legs and runny noses, to thaw out by the fire.

Perhaps my most vivid memory of that time is of Guy Fawkes night in 1935. My father had gone to a great deal of trouble, building an enormous bonfire in the garden and topping it off with a man-sized guy made from one of his old suits, which had been stuffed with paper. This guy was finished off with a grotesque mask (bought on a recent trip to Aylesbury) which terrified me. Nevertheless I looked forward to the spectacle promised by Dad on the 5th of November.

That night, anticipating a great display, I watched along with Mum, Mike and our new Red Setter puppy, Sandy, as my father lit the bonfire. Then, as the flames began to lick around the feet of the guy, Dad lit one of several Catherine wheels fixed at strategic points around the garden. The wheel began to spin on its nail, slowly at first and then, gathering momentum, it leapt from its post in a trail of sparks, landing in the box of fireworks lying open on the ground. Suddenly, bangers exploded everywhere and rockets flew off in all directions. My father dived for cover behind a bush, while Mum pulled Mike, Sandy and me out of danger behind the house. The noise eventually subsided and we emerged again to see Dad – his hair singed at the front – staring mournfully down at the charred remains of the box. Mum saw the disappointment on our faces and began to give him a ticking-off which turned quickly into a fit of hysterical, mutual giggling. It was rare to see them laughing together and this is probably why I remember the incident so well.

In 1936 my father announced that we were going to move to London. He had found a job as a window-cleaner with the Wandsworth Borough Council and explained that the promise of regular employment had convinced him that the move would be a wise one. In later years I discovered that he had in fact been forced to sell the cottage – for £100 – in order to settle several urgent debts in the village.

A few days later, with the help of two removal men, we loaded all our belongings into the back of the furniture van he had hired for the move. In the back of the van, between bedsteads, tea-chests and a sideboard, Mum, Mike and I took a firm grip on the tailboard while Sandy whimpered beside us. We stuck our heads over the top to wave good-bye to our grandparents and the few neighbours who had stayed to see us off. There was a grinding of gears and the van lurched forward, so beginning the first long journey of my life.

An hour or so later the van was rolling through the outskirts of the city and to me, a young, impressionable country boy used only to green fields, thatched cottages and wide-open spaces, London seemed a huge and improbable place. We passed row upon row of terraced streets and I saw more people, houses, cars, horses and carts than I had previously seen in the whole of my life. The van eventually turned into a narrow street in Balham, where it shuddered to a halt outside our new home.

That evening, when we had carried all our belongings into the flat, Mum tucked Mike and me into our large double-bed but, tired though we were, it was impossible to sleep amid the strange new sounds in the darkness, with the bumps and bangs from the flat above and the noise of people talking out in the street. And there were things in the bed with us, things that bit at our arms and legs.

Next morning we discovered what these things were. As we all sat wearily down to breakfast my father told us that the flat was infested with bugs. Mum was disgusted at the thought of having to call in the pest exterminators and I think we all seriously doubted the wisdom of our move to London.

But when the bugs had gone and Mum had made the flat spick and span, when Dad settled into his new job, and when Mike and I found new friends in the street, we began to grow accustomed to city life, although our financial situation was little better than it had been in the country. Mum and I often hid behind the front-room curtains while the rent-collector rapped loudly on the front door. Then he would shake his head, turn the page in his tally-book then walk away, and we could breathe easily once more – until the next week. But soon we were on the move again, just a few miles down the road to a basement flat in Pendennis Road, Streatham.

In 1939 my father was promoted to the post of caretaker at the Public Library in Disraeli Road, Putney. We moved into the house adjoining the library and began to look forward to a more financially secure life. But, like every other family in the country our lives were soon disrupted by an event even more momentous than the Depression – the outbreak of war.

For Mike and I the early days of the war meant intermittent journeys between London and our grandparents' home in Oving, where it was assumed we would be safe from the bombing raids. Mum put us on the train at Marylebone and Grandad Fincher met us in Aylesbury; but it was the journey itself that I enjoyed the best. It was the first time I had travelled anywhere without one or other of my parents, and I felt an enormous sense of freedom as I watched the white smoke from the train drift across the open countryside. Unfortunately my 'freedom' lasted only until our arrival in Aylesbury where Grandad waited for us, determined we would not run wild while in his care.

I was a cheeky kid, typical of the time, with an 'S' belt holding up my baggy shorts and a runny nose wiped every so often on my sleeve. In fact, I was described by a teacher at the village school as being her idea of William, the character created by Richmal Crompton. I hated school and was never much of a scholar. As the afternoons dragged interminably on, I could hardly wait for the singing of the hymn which had these words:

The day thou gavest, Lord, is ended,
The darkness falls at thy behest . . .

and which signalled the end of the school day.

Most of the village children – evacuees and locals – became involved in a scheme called 'Cogs-in-the-Wheel', run by the Women's Voluntary Service. We were given a badge to wear, showing that we were cogs-in-the-wheel of the war effort. Our part in the fight against the foe was to go around the village and collect as much wastepaper as possible which would then be taken away for re-cycling.

After one collection, Mike sat me on top of the pile of paper on a four-wheeled barrow, and gave me a hefty shove down Parrotts Hill. The barrow gathered speed and I didn't dare to jump off, so I clung on tightly until it came to a halt by crashing into the front door of a house at the bottom of the hill. Wastepaper flew everywhere and the lady of the house came out to yell at me while Mike and my mates ran off to hide behind the churchyard wall. Grandad got to hear of the incident and promised me a belting if it happened again.

A few days later the same barrow was standing empty at the top of Oving Hill, just outside the village. There were no houses on or near this hill, so there was little danger of an accident like the last one. Despite Grandad's warning the temptation was too great and climbing onto the barrow again I told my friends to give me a shove. The truck went even faster this time and the risk, I thought, was well worth it – until I passed my grim-faced grandfather pushing his bicycle in the opposite direction. He had to step sharply aside to let me pass and when I got home I got the belting I'd been promised.

One Whitsuntide, a friend and I were taking a walk through some fields when we came across an unforgettable sight: a respected gentleman of the village was having fun and games with a Land Army girl in a hayrick. Fascinated, we watched for a while then sneaked off without disturbing the happy couple. But our curiosity about matters sexual was aroused.

As the villagers prepared for the Whit-Fete in the sports field my friends and I, with the object of finding out a bit more about the mysteries of womanhood, enticed a rather gullible girl – an evacuee, like us – beneath one of the trestle tables. We asked her to give us a look, but she refused until I offered to give her a halfpenny. Only then did she lift her skirt, to reveal skinny white legs and a pair of navy-blue knickers. Suddenly they were down. But my friend and I hardly had time to lean closer for a proper inspection before they were up again. The girl grabbed the halfpenny then darted out from under the table.

On the way home my friend and I decided we'd been conned and put it down to experience. Unfortunately that was not the end of the matter. The girl was convinced she would have a baby because two boys had looked at her 'down there'. She ran home and confessed all to her guardian, a stern-looking woman who was waiting for us at the garden gate with my grandmother. They marched us into the front-room and proceeded to lecture us on morality for the next half-hour. We were alternately laughing and crying throughout the tirade and almost collapsed in hysterics when the girl was called in from the kitchen to tell her side of the story. We emerged embarrassed and tearful from the ordeal and became the butt of jokes from other village boys for weeks to come.

There came a time when it was considered safe for us to return to Putney. By then Mike was growing into a young man and increasingly frustrated by the fact that he was still too young to join the forces. Eventually he lied about his age and joined the Royal Navy. He was posted to the Far East and I did not see him again for almost three years. My father, too, went away when he was called up into the Army, although he did manage to get home on leave most weekends; Mum worked all day at the Army and Navy Stores in Victoria. Their combined absence meant I was able to play hookey from school with my pals, without the likelihood of getting caught.

The world became a more violent place, and in a way we became hardened to the daily news of bombing and killing. To be honest, London was a very exciting place for all young boys during the war. Life was never dull. We often caught a bus up to Piccadilly where we would ask passing American soldiers if they had 'any gum, chum?' and we used to hang around the famous 'Stage Door' canteen, hoping to catch a glimpse of visiting American film stars. We fought our own little wars, building 'tanks' out of old orange boxes and filling bottles with methylated spirit to use as bombs! After air-raids we would pick up unexploded incendiary bombs as though they were harmless sticks of wood, then dismantle them in the library cellar. Once we found a huge firework and, naturally, we took it down to the river, stuck it in the mud by the towpath and lit it. The result was spectacular. The entire embankment was illuminated for about two minutes and the local ARP unit thought another air-raid had begun!

But we were not immune from the tragedy of war. One Sunday evening a bomb fell very close to the library. As it exploded, my father, home on week-end leave, leapt over the back of the settee yelling: 'Christ! That was close!' He went out to see what had happened and discovered that the bomb had fallen on a local dance hall. He returned hours later, having helped in the rescue, his clothes covered in dust and smeared with blood. Over a hundred young people, some of them Mike's friends, had been killed in the raid.

One Thursday, the Germans began sending a new kind of bomb across the North Sea in yet another attempt to destroy London: the V1 flying-bombs or 'doodle-bugs' as they soon became known.

At the time I had a job as a paper-boy, delivering for a large newsagent in the High Street. I was supplied with a red bicycle which I was allowed to use in my own time, and my 'round' covered the streets down by the Thames to the west of Putney Bridge. One Saturday afternoon I cycled over to Clapham Junction with my friend Bobby Jones – another paper-boy – to see the damage done by a flying bomb near the Granada Cinema there, and we spent an exciting hour or so watching the wardens and firemen searching for bodies in the rubble.

Early next morning Bobby and I sorted out our bundles of Sunday papers as usual, shoved them into our bags, and arranged to meet up later. As I pushed off down the High Street I glanced back to see him pedalling towards the start of his round in Norry Road. I had almost reached the bridge when the air-raid sirens howled out their familiar warning and, above them, I heard the droning sound of a flying-bomb. I looked up and saw its bullet-like shape over the flats on the embankment. I ditched my bike on the

pavement. The papers spilled out onto the ground as I ran with several other people down the stone steps of the Gents' toilet built into the wall of the bridge. The noise of the bomb stopped abruptly. A few seconds passed and then it exploded somewhere very close.

When the noise subsided, I climbed the steps again, picked up my bike, stuffed the papers back in the bag and began to make my way back home, fearing the worst – that the bomb had landed on the library, killing my mother.

It was impossible to see the top end of the High Street, shrouded as it was in a thick cloud of dust and since every shop window had been shattered by the blast, covering the road and pavements with broken glass, I had to push my bike all the way home. Thankfully the library was still intact, but Mum was nowhere to be seen. I went to look for her in Norry Road as she often went that way on Sunday mornings to a greengrocer's shop.

As I ran into Norry Road it was immediately obvious that the bomb had landed there. Several houses had been destroyed and policemen and wardens were trying to organize the rescue and calm people down at the same time. Local Civil Defence rescue vehicles were arriving and bodies were already being pulled out of the rubble. I tried to get a closer look but an ARP warden turned me away. Then, much to my relief, I saw my mother.

She was standing with Bobby's mother and his sister, and they were all weeping. Mum took me aside and told me that Bobby had been killed in the explosion.

Bobby Jones's funeral was held a few days later at Roehampton Vale Cemetery and I attended with four other boys who had known him, too. We walked solemnly along behind the black, old-fashioned hearse which carried the small, boy-sized coffin. Staring into the polished metal at the back of the vehicle, we caught our own reflections looking nervously back at us, distorted by the curve of the metal like the funny mirrors in a fairground. One of us sniggered, unable to hold it in. Someone else pulled a funny face and suddenly we were all giggling. This suppressed nervous merriment lasted until we stood at the bus stop opposite the cemetery gates, waiting to go home on a No. 85 bus. Only then did the laughter stop and turn spontaneously into uncontrollable tears.

With the lack of regular paternal discipline at home, my mother began to worry about my upbringing; she feared that I might be 'going off the rails' and mixing with the 'wrong sort'. So she enrolled me at Clark's College in Putney, in the hope that I would absorb some middle-class manners, and better myself in the process. Unfortunately this was a sad miscalculation on her part, for I was one of the college's least successful pupils and was easily distracted, particularly during maths. The height of my achievements at Clark's College was the threat of expulsion after flicking ink-soaked balls of blotting-paper onto the newly decorated ceiling of a classroom. I was soon transferred back to an LCC school.

It was around this time that I caught the photography 'bug'. It happened when my mother took me to visit an old gentlemen named Mr Sainsbury who lived just a few doors away from the library. He was an enthusiastic amateur photographer who would proudly display his collection of cameras and prints to anyone who would look at them. He demonstrated an old wooden contact printer for me, and I watched fascinated as the image magically appeared on a sheet cf bromide paper in a dish of chemicals. After that I went to see Mr Sainsbury several times, eager to learn all I could about photography.

I bought a small contact printer and some packets of powdered chemicals and began to experiment in the library cellar with some old negatives he had given me. Photography seemed relatively easy compared to the complexities of school and college, and it had the added bonus of being something my friends knew nothing about. I was able to impress them with my new-found skills as I showed them the prints I had made in the cellar.

At that time there were a number of 'newspaper' films showing at the local cinema, in which reporters would rush into the news-room at the last minute, yelling, 'Hold the front page!' I sat through these films as many times as I could, soaking up their atmosphere and excitement. It wasn't long before my ambitions were clearly defined: I wanted to become a *great* press photographer and I wanted to work for a *great* newspaper – it was as simple as that.

3

Learning the Trade

My first job after leaving school in 1945 had nothing whatsoever to do with photography or newspapers. I became an electrician's mate in a large wholesale clothing company, based near St Paul's Churchyard. During my lunch-breaks, wearing my greasy overalls, I would wander along nearby Fleet Street, and dream. I used to gaze up at the offices of famous newspapers and try to imagine the scenes inside. Often I'd stand on the steps and watch the people coming and going. One day I saw a photographer rushing off to an assignment somewhere; he was carrying a large plate camera with a flashlight attached, the kind of camera I was itching to get my hands on. I realized I had to do something fast, and that evening I told my mother of my ambition. I don't know how she did it but a few days later she had arranged an appointment for me at Keystone.

After a short interview with the Company Secretary, Tom Newman, I was told that I had a job as a messenger-boy – at 18s 6d per week. I gladly handed in my notice at the clothing firm and began working for Keystone about a week later.

There were several messengers, all of us important to the success of the agency. We sat on a long wooden bench in the despatch office, waiting for the plates to be brought in, either by despatch-rider or by the photographers themselves.

When the plates arrived a kind of mad panic took over the place. They were developed immediately and the pictures were printed and dried in less than 15 minutes. The drying operation was particularly dangerous; it involved soaking each print in a dish of methylated spirit, blotting it off with newspaper and then holding it over a lighted gas-ring. Many fringes and eyebrows were sacrificed to this process, as prints would often catch fire when held too close to the flame.

The pictures were then captioned and handed to us with the command: 'Rush! Rush!' And off we'd rush, to all the newspapers in Fleet Street, starting with the three evening papers the *Star*, *News* and *Standard*; then came the dailies and the provincial papers with offices in Fleet Street. Speed was of the essence as we were competing against all the other agencies who had often covered exactly the same stories – agencies like Sport and General, Topical, INP, Planet, Barratts and Central Press, to name a few.

I covered many miles in an average day and in all kinds of weather. Unfortunately I had just one pair of shoes, a cheap pair which wore thin very quickly. I had to put cardboard in the soles to keep out the wet but nothing could dampen my enthusiasm for I was caught up in the magic of Fleet Street. There was something very special about being inside the great newspaper offices, just as I had always imagined there would be during my lunch-time wanderings.

Every now and then I would be sent out on assignments with photographers, to carry their cameras for them and rush back to the office with urgent plates while they stayed on to continue their coverage.

One of my favourite Keystone photographers was Fred Ramage. I would listen in rapt fascination as he recounted the tales of his days as a war photographer and I wondered if I'd ever have such stories of my own to tell.

The atmosphere of bustling, important activity coupled with the smell of printer's ink spurred me on towards bigger and better things. I became keener than any of the other messenger-boys. I was willing to work early in the morning or till late at night without complaint and my eagerness was soon recognized by the Keystone management. I was promoted to the glazing-room.

As a reward for my efforts my mother bought me an old folding camera – for 18*s* 6*d* – from the City Sale Exchange in Fleet Street, and I began taking pictures from that day on.

Two operations took place in the glazing-room. The 'rush' prints were dried via the 'meths' method, and prints for distribution to magazines etc., which were not so urgent, were glazed on a huge chromium-plated drum. This was a tricky job: if the operator paid too little attention many precious prints could shrivel up on the heated metal and be destroyed forever. I believe Larry Burrows was sacked from Keystone a few years earlier for just such a mistake and I was certain I'd receive the same fate when I unwittingly set the 'meths' on fire one morning, at the same time scorching the trousers of my immediate boss, John Stean. There was a

row about who was to blame for the fire and I was sent home. I told my mother that my prospects of a successful Fleet Street career had vanished in a puff of smoke. At lunchtime, well aware that the fire had been my fault, I telephoned George Pratt and apologized for the mishap. 'Well, boy, you'd better come back in and we'll sort it out,' he said. Much to my surprise John Stean put in a good word for me and I was reprieved, with a warning to be more careful in future.

I was soon promoted again. This time I became a chemical-boy, responsible for developing some of the plates and mixing all the chemicals used in the darkroom. Sometimes, in the winter, when the developer was cold and the plates took a bit too long 'coming through', we employed an old trick of the trade, a simple matter of urinating into the dish. It never failed to raise the temperature and the plates of many famous pictures have been helped along by this method!

We were often visited in the darkroom by a once-famous photographer named Ernest Brooks, an elegantly dressed old chap who had been known as 'The Royal Photographer' because of his past association with several members of the Royal family. Unfortunately he had fallen on hard times and was now forced to make money wherever he could. He would often walk in the Royal Parks, stopping to photograph nannies with the children in their care, later selling these small prints for a few pennies each. One day he came into the darkroom with a very smart pair of his old trousers to sell. I bought them for two shillings and wore them next day.

As I sat – with my camera in my lap – on a No. 14 bus on my way to work, I spotted our local policeman, PC Wilcox, holding up the traffic and shepherding a swan across Putney Bridge. I leapt off the bus and photographed the scene. I developed the plate as soon as I got to work and the picture was sold to all three evening papers. It was my first publication and I felt on top of the world. After that 'Brooks's lucky trousers' became a great joke around the office and I

My first published picture

wore them for months to come, until they literally fell apart.

I soon moved up another step in the profession when I became a developer-boy under the watchful eye of Tom Bunt, the chief printer. Tom was a short man who bore a remarkable resemblance to the famous cartoon character, Popeye. A cigarette dangled constantly from his lips and its ash dropped onto his overalls whenever he spoke. His finger-nails had turned dark brown after years of dipping them into the developer, an occupational hazard. He worked a horizontal enlarger, a crude apparatus by today's standards, with a 'tin lid' over the lens which he would flip off at the moment of exposure. He was the fastest printer I ever knew, with an uncanny knack for getting the exposure right every time on a long run. Unfortunately, Tom's assistants were not all as expert as he was. We were apt to ruin his perfect timing by leaving a print too long in the developer, or by not 'fixing' it properly. Whenever a print was ruined the culprit would get a wallop round the ear from him, usually with a box of photographic papers.

But Tom had the proverbial heart of gold. He taught me, and several others who went on to become successful Fleet Street photographers, all he knew about printing pictures. He also gave me guidance as a photographer, suggesting that I spend my lunch-breaks taking pictures around the city. I took his advice and every so often my photographs would appear in the evening papers, earning me a pound a time.

One lunch-time I was photographing the flowers growing among the rubble of the bomb ruins in the old Temple grounds, when a woman tapped me on the shoulder. 'That's who you ought to be taking pictures of, young man,' she said, pointing to a rather elegant looking couple strolling in the grounds.

'Why, who are they?' I asked.

'Don't you know?' replied the woman scornfully. 'The man is Ivor Novello and the lady is Greta Garbo.'

I wasn't too sure who Ivor Novello was, but I knew all about Greta Garbo, the legendary film star who shunned publicity, and it didn't take me long to realize that I had a 'scoop' in the making. While trying to smarten myself up by straightening out my shabby, chemical-stained clothes as best I could, I approached the famous couple.

'Excuse me, Miss Garbo, Mr Novello, but may I photograph you both?' I asked in my best Sunday voice.

They both looked me up and down and before they had a chance to tell me to get lost, I continued with a touch of pathos: 'You've no idea what a great help it would be to my career.'

They looked me up and down again and decided, presumably from the look of me, that my career needed all the help it could get, and they agreed to pose for me.

By this time my old camera had seen a lot of use. Its back had worked loose and was held on with sticky tape. I couldn't afford the correct plates to fit my slides and was making do with odd bits of film that I had cut down to size in the darkroom. In my nervousness the first two sheets of film blew away in the breeze, but I did manage to expose the remaining three. I thanked the famous couple profusely then rushed back to Keystone proclaiming my great 'scoop'.

George Pratt, having heard about it, emerged from his office. He knew the pictures would be successful and a feather in Keystone's cap. He took my slides and handed them to Tom, telling him to rush them through, while I sat back, waiting to bask in the praise that must surely follow.

After what seemed an age Tom came out of the darkroom, with my negatives in his hands, but he wasn't smiling as I'd expected him to be. He held the developed film up to the light and in front of George and me. All three were fogged with black streaks and there wasn't the remotest image of a famous film star on any of them. Somehow, light had seeped in through the back of my crude camera and I blushed to the roots of my hair.

George muttered something about missing a 'scoop' and Fred Ramage gave me some advice which I have never forgotten. 'Never shout about your pictures, son,' he said, 'until they're developed and printed.'

During the late forties and early fifties I mixed with a South London gang known as the Elephant Boys. They were a bunch of tough, young tearaways from the Elephant and Castle district and since I came from Putney I regarded it as something of an honour to be numbered among them. For some, their period spent with the gang was a kind of apprenticeship for big-time crime. I was there just for the fun of it.

For the Elephant Boys week-ends were for dancing and punch-ups. Our battle-grounds were the local dance-halls and we were often involved in fights with rival gangs from north of the river. I remember quite vividly one Saturday night at the Wimbledon Palais when the vast dance-floor was cleared by a pitched-battle between us and another gang. But somehow the bandleader, Ken MacKintosh, bravely managed to keep a jaunty foxtrot playing while bodies, chairs and bottles clattered all around his rostrum.

Usually, while the last waltz was being danced, we would head for the nearest tea and coffee stall to drink cups of hot tea and eat steak-and-kidney pies smothered in rich brown sauce. Then it was off to a West End jazz club until the early hours of Sunday morning when we would stagger home to catch up on some sleep before setting out again for the afternoon's film at the local cinema. On Sunday evening it was up to the Lyceum in the Strand for more dancing, usually to Harry Roy and his music.

I renewed my friendship with Gordon Goody, a tough character I had known since my late schooldays. In turn, Gordon became friendly with Charlie Wilson, another pal of mine, from Battersea. Theirs turned out to be a fateful friendship for they both became key members of the gang eventually known as the 'Great Train Robbers'. My own interests lay firmly in the world of photography and were enough to keep me on the straight and narrow.

*

One evening in 1953 I went to the Star and Garter, a pub on the embankment in Putney, for a drink with an old school-friend, Terry Acutt. He had arranged to meet a girl there and kept telling me how lovely she was. That day I had been on a rather glamorous assignment, to photograph the dancers at the famous Windmill Theatre in Soho. I had one of the prints in my pocket and was kidding Terry that it was a picture of my latest girl-friend, when his date arrived. She was a tall, fair-haired girl whom he introduced as June Smith.

I thought she might be an actress or a model for she was certainly every bit as lovely as any of the girls I had photographed earlier that day. In fact, her rather elegant appearance put me off a bit and somehow undermined my rough confidence so that soon I found myself talking too much. In an effort to impress, I even showed her the picture of the Windmill girl, but June was not impressed and the evening ended on a rather flat note for me when she left with Terry.

Some months later, at a dance in the Wimbledon Palais, I saw her again and asked her to dance. At first she refused but then agreed when she remembered me as Terry's friend. I was never much of a Fred Astaire, my modest limits on the dance floor extending only as far as the waltz or the fox-trot. Luckily Ken MacKintosh's band was playing a slow foxtrot, and I was able to begin my big chat-up routine with confidence. In one of the more intimate moments of the dance I tried to kiss June's ear, my favourite approach, gleaned from Hollywood movies. She didn't respond as I had hoped and I thought I had lost my chance with her. When the music stopped I knew I had to do something quickly to save the situation, so I told her quite bluntly that I fancied her. To my relief this remark brought the first of many understanding smiles to her lips. I asked if I might photo-graph her some time. She agreed, and our relationship was at last off to a fine start.

I began to pay regular visits to June's home near the gasworks in Fairfield Street, Wandsworth, where she lived with her mother and her sister, Rose. Her Mum

would always invite me to Sunday lunch, but I didn't make a very good impression with her on my second visit when I had to ask her to lend me the bus fare home.

June and I became engaged and we planned to get married in March 1955. At the beginning of the year Keystone offered me a posting to Paris, but when they learned of my wedding plans they withdrew the offer. We were married on 19 March 1955, in the Wandsworth Register Office. The ceremony was followed by a 'knees-up' in her Mum's front-room and afterwards we left for a week-end honeymoon at the Bull Hotel in Aylesbury. We began married life in a fur-nished room in Wandsworth but eventually moved to our comfortable attic flat in Sydenham.

Since our brief encounter in the Star and Garter, June has given me three lovely daughters – Jayne, Sally and Lucy. She has packed my bags and driven me to the airport many times, often seeing me off to the trou-ble spots of the world, never knowing if I'd return home again. She has shared my fears and listened patiently to my problems. Jour-nalists may seem tough on the outside but, believe me, all the successful ones have a core of sensitivity and compassion which, affected by some harrowing assignment, can drive many to seek solace in the contents of a bottle while some may find other methods of drifting away from reality. I'm lucky. June is my anchor.

I stayed with Keystone until late 1957 when, because of my increasing success following the Suez crisis, I began to grow restless. I wanted to achieve another great ambition by working on a national newspaper. Hearing of a vacancy on the *Daily Herald* I con-tacted Len Hickman, the Picture Editor, and explained my feelings to him. In turn, Len arranged an interview for me with the Deputy Editor, Geoff Pinnington. Geoff offered me the job at £25 per week and I was delighted to accept. Between the time of the interview and the date I was due to join the

Onlookers at a Society wedding, London, 1955

June

Chelsea Baby Show, 1957

38

Herald, I won the Press Photographer of the Year Award and, as a result, Geoff Pinnington gave me a rise of £2 per week before I had taken a single picture for his paper. I had been very happy at Keystone; I'd learned a lot there and despite looking forward to an exciting career with the *Herald*, I was sorry to leave the photo agency.

I stayed with the *Daily Herald* until 1961 when I moved to the *Daily Express*, with whom I was to spend the next eight hectic, but happy, years. In 1969, after a very brief spell of freelancing, I joined the new *Sun*, but found that my short period of 'freedom' had made it impossible for me to settle again as a staff man so I left, after just three weeks.

Eventually I formed my own agency, Photographers International, which today syndicates my work world-wide.

Photo-journalism must be *the* most unpredictable of professions. One day a photographer might find himself shooting pictures of a glamorous model and on the next he could be amid the gory horrors of a war on the other side of the world. Since it would prove very confusing to attempt to present the curious ebb and flow of a photo-journalist's life in any chronological sequence, the following chapters deal separately with the various themes I have encountered during 25 years of feeding the hungry monster whose heart beats in Fleet Street.

4

Crime and Punishment

It was on the pavement outside an estate agent's office in Gloucester Road, in March 1949, that I was first initiated into the fascinating world of crime reporting. Inside the office Scotland Yard detectives were searching for clues in the case of 'The Acid Bath Murder', in which John George Haigh had admitted to shooting a wealthy widow, Mrs Durand-Deacon, and then dissolving her body in a tank filled with sulphuric acid. Haigh also claimed to have disposed of several other bodies by the same method and I believe it was in connection with this aspect of the case that the detectives had been sent to Gloucester Road.

I was a cheeky 17-year-old at the time, still working in the Keystone darkroom. On that particular day, however, there must have been a lot of newsworthy happenings around London because the agency were short of photographers to cover assignments. I had been told to stop my work and take my camera along to Gloucester Road and watch the estate agent's office. Even though I was wearing chemical-stained clothes and was equipped only with my 18s 6d camera, I stood there quite confidently alongside the elite of Fleet Street's crime reporters and photographers. These were

men who specialized in the world of intrigue; they wore soft felt trilbies, their overcoat collars were turned up, they all spoke in whispers out of the side of their mouths and they were on first-name terms with the detectives. I was greatly impressed.

I pushed my way to the front where a photographer, hiding his plate camera under his coat, turned to me and asked: 'Where are you from, sonny?'

I took objection to this, but politely informed him that I represented Keystone. He grunted and took no more notice of me. He was Bill Malindine of the *Daily Mirror* who would, in later years, become a good friend, often helping me out on other crime stories – for help is vital in this essentially clannish side of the business.

That day I watched the comings and goings of the detectives, but produced nothing out of the story and soon found myself back behind the developing dishes in the darkroom.

It seemed to me that, in the early fifties, there was nothing the British public enjoyed more than reading a good murder story in the newspapers. This was, of course, well before the abolition of the death penalty and each one of these stories carried the added ingredient of the possible hanging of the murderer.

In those days London's newspaper-sellers really did call out: '*Star*, *News* and *Standard* – Read all about it!', a cry usually followed by the day's headlines. One that I particularly remember, because I covered the story, was: '*Star*, *News* and *Standard* – Read all about it . . . Lady in Red Shoes Murdered in Soho!' The lady in question was a prostitute killed in a Soho flat. Once again I stood in the street, shoulder to shoulder with the Fleet Street heavy brigade, and once again I produced nothing worthy of publication. (I can't even recall the date now but that newspaper-seller's cry sticks in my mind.)

The first murder story I covered in rather more depth was the controversial Craig and Bentley case in the winter of 1953. Nineteen-year-old Derek Bentley and his accomplice, Christopher Craig, who was only 16, broke into a warehouse in Croydon. They were spotted entering the building and the police were informed. The two boys were hiding on the rooftop when they were confronted by a detective. Bentley gave himself up. Meanwhile police reinforcements were arriving and when the first constable appeared on the roof, Bentley is said to have shouted, 'Let him have it, Chris!' Craig, who was carrying a revolver, shot the constable in the head, killing him instantly and then leapt off the roof, landing badly on the ground and injuring his spine.

After their trial at the Old Bailey both boys were found guilty of murder, but Craig – who had actually fired the shot – was, according to prevalent English law, too young to hang and he was sentenced to be 'detained at Her Majesty's pleasure'. Bentley, whom the prosecution claimed had encouraged the shooting by calling out at the crucial moment (but whose defence rested

William Bentley, father of Derek Bentley, with Mrs Craig, mother of Christopher Craig, in the ABC Cafe, Whitehall

on the contention that, 'Let him have it, Chris' had been advice to hand over the gun), was sentenced to death.

A public outcry followed, owing to the seeming inequality of the sentences, and Bentley's father and sister, along with Craig's mother, went to the Home Office to plead with the Home Secretary, Sir David Maxwell-Fyfe for the sentence to be commuted to life imprisonment. In the few days before the execution was due to take place, I was assigned to follow them and record their progress. As we sat together, sipping tea in the ABC cafe in Whitehall, the Bentleys were hopeful of success but within a few hours they learned it had all been for nothing. The sentence remained.

On the eve of their son's execution I waited outside Wandsworth Prison as Bentley's parents went inside to see him for the last time. Half an hour later they came out again, a frail, broken-hearted couple. Mrs Bentley was in a state of near collapse and something about her vulnerability reminded me of my own mother. For the first time in my career I lowered my camera, unable to take a picture.

Next morning I was given the depressing task of photographing the crowd scenes outside the prison. Morbid curiosity always accounted for many of the spectators, who turned out to wait by prison gates while an execution took place inside. The anti-hanging faction were also there, offering up a prayer. Several angry people tried to tear down Bentley's death notice, fixed to the gate. But, by then, it was too late.

In March I was sent to No. 10 Rillington Place, Notting Hill, where the dead body of a naked woman had been found in a hidden cupboard. No. 10 was a dingy little house at the end of a dismal cul-de-sac. It was already a notorious address, having been the home of Timothy Evans, a Welshman who, in 1949, had been convicted and hanged for the murder of his baby daughter. The police announced that they were now looking for John Reginald Halliday Christie, the former tenant, who had figured strongly in the case against Evans.

Meanwhile they were searching every inch of the place and on the day I arrived, the body of Mrs Christie was discovered beneath the floor-boards in the living-room.

Next morning the police began to excavate the back garden. Another photographer and I quickly agreed to share the expense of renting a room overlooking the rear of the house. We settled down at the window with our cameras trained on the scene, and watched several plain-clothes detectives busily digging up the soil. Throughout the day they unearthed several objects which they wrapped carefully in pieces of cloth before sending them away for examination. In all the remains of two female bodies were exhumed from the garden.

The hunt for Christie became more urgent. His picture appeared in all the papers and the headlines screamed: WHEN WILL THE KILLER STRIKE AGAIN? He was reportedly seen in country districts but no one had been able to confirm a positive sighting.

At the time I was living alone in a small flat in Werter Road, Putney (having moved out of the library as my father and I had not been getting along since my demobilization). Each day, throughout my coverage of the story, I travelled back and forth to Notting Hill by bus and tube, keeping my camera ready and my eyes peeled, constantly searching for a glimpse of Christie.

At 8 o'clock on the morning of 31 March I had crossed Putney Bridge, on the way to Rillington Place once more. Shortly after 9 o'clock a police constable spotted a shabby little man leaning on the Embankment railings about a hundred yards from the bridge (not far from the gents' toilet where I had dived for cover from the flying-bomb nine years earlier). The constable asked the man to remove his hat, then realized he was staring into the face of Christie. Britain's most wanted man of the day went quietly with the policeman to Putney police station. The hunt had ended just a quarter of a mile from my flat.

I continued to cover the story of Reginald Christie for several weeks, still hoping to get a picture of him. After several appearances at the West London Magistrates' Court, near Olympia, he was taken to Brixton Prison to await trial. I attended a preliminary hearing held for some obscure reason at Clerkenwell Juvenile Court. The place was packed with people, including several over-dressed 'ladies' with rouged cheeks and garish lipstick painted a little too high on their lips who sat in the public gallery, their attention riveted on Christie's pathetic, gnome-like figure.

Photography is strictly prohibited in any English court or its precincts. In the case of Christie I was restricted to the usual practice of waiting outside, camera at the ready, in the hope that when he left the various hearings under escort on the way back to prison, I might catch him without the familiar blanket covering his head. But it was not to be.

Christie was finally found guilty of the murder of his wife. He also confessed to killing five other women. He was duly executed at Pentonville Prison on 15 July 1953, the same prison in which Timothy Evans had met his end four years earlier.

In the light of evidence gathered during Christie's trial two government inquiries into the case against Evans took place during the following 12 years. Towards the end of the second inquiry in October 1966, I re-visited Rillington Place to illustrate a *Daily Express* article on the case. Following this inquiry Evans was given a free pardon, 16 years after his execution. Rillington Place no longer exists. The street was demolished to make way for a motorway.

As Jim Callaghan urged the House of Commons towards the abolition of the death

A body is removed from No. 10 Rillington Place

penalty in 1969, I was assigned to photograph the former public executioner Albert Pierrepoint to illustrate a *Sun* feature on the debate. I arrived at Pierrepoint's home early one frosty December morning. As I rang the doorbell I wondered what sort of man I was about to meet. He had sent more than 400 people to their death at the end of a rope. Included among his more famous 'clients' were: the war-time traitor, William Joyce (better known as 'Lord Haw-Haw'), convicted murderers Heath, Haigh, Christie – and Ruth Ellis, the last woman to hang in Britain. Pierrepoint had retired from office shortly after the Ruth Ellis affair, but claimed that her death and public reaction to it had nothing to do with his decision to quit.

I soon found myself shaking hands with a warm, friendly man who took me inside his comfortable home, where his wife was waiting with a welcoming cup of tea. We passed the time of day looking at his collection of family photographs, then he asked me where I wanted to take his picture. I told him I'd spotted a suitable location nearby, a bare tree which looked like an old 'hanging tree'. He agreed and as I was taking the picture we spoke about the campaign. 'I can't say much,' he said, 'but I do hope Jim Callaghan gets his way.'

Albert Pierrepoint, former public executioner

Jim Callaghan did get his way. Capital punishment was abolished soon afterwards.

On a pleasant spring morning in 1963 I found myself 'door-stepping' Sir Winston Churchill at his home near Hyde Park Gate, where he had recently recovered from an illness.

Door-stepping is the single most tedious chore in the newspaper world, consisting of nothing more than waiting in the street outside the home or hideout or whatever of a particular newsworthy subject, in the hope of grabbing an up-to-the-minute picture of him or her. This assignment had so far dragged on for almost two weeks and Sir Winston hadn't so much as peeped through the curtains. However, on this particular morning the monotony was relieved somewhat by the arrival of another photographer, Terry O'Neill, given the same assignment by his paper, the *Daily Sketch*. Once again it became a long and fruitless wait, and by mid-afternoon Terry and I were well and truly fed-up. We decided to take a stroll across Kensington Gore and into the park for a cup of tea and a sandwich.

As we approached a cafeteria by the Serpentine, I spotted a couple of familiar faces among the people enjoying the spring sunshine. One of them was Gordon Goody. Gordon and I had kept in touch since our teenage days together and he often visited my home, staying for tea on several occasions. His last visit had been a couple of months earlier. The other face in the crowd belonged to Charlie Wilson, whom I had not seen for a year or more.

It was apparent that Gordon and Charlie were in the company of several other men. They'd pulled a couple of tables together and some of them were just lounging back in their chairs while others fed breadcrumbs to the sparrows and pigeons.

I approached Gordon and said 'Hello', but he was ill-at-ease as we shook hands, and not his usual, friendly self. Several of his companions eyed our cameras suspiciously, as I introduced him to Terry. I greeted Charlie, who also had an air of uneasiness about

him, although he did buy a cup of tea each for Terry and myself. Neither of my old friends introduced me to any of the other men – none of whom I recognized – and both seemed relieved when I said we had to return to the job of Churchill-watching.

I thought no more about this strange meeting in the park with Gordon and Charlie, until they were later both arrested in connection with the Great Train Robbery.

I had returned in August 1963 from an assignment abroad, and read with amazement the story of the robbery in which a staggering £2,600,000 had been stolen in a well-organized military-style raid on a night mail train, as it headed southwards along a lonely stretch of track at Sears Crossing, in Buckinghamshire.

In the months that followed, several other members of the gang were tracked down and arrested. In April the following year, men whose names had become familiar to the entire nation – Ronnie Biggs, James Hussey, Roy James, Robert Welch, William Boal, Roger Cordey, Buster Edwards, Brian Field, Tom Wisbey and Bruce Reynolds – all appeared, with my two old friends, before Mr Justice Edmund Davies in a makeshift courtroom at Aylesbury. All were given massive sentences.

The thieves had won the grudging admiration of millions of ordinary law-abiding citizens and had soon attained a Robin Hood-like celebrity for the daring way in which they had carried out the robbery.

As they languished in prison cells dotted about the country, escape plans were hatched. Several members of the gang managed to flee the country, only to find themselves hotly pursued by Superintendent Thomas Butler of Scotland Yard. In 1964 Charlie Wilson escaped from Birmingham's Winson Green Prison and I was to hear no more of him until one cold Thursday morning in January 1968.

That morning I was lying in bed reading the day's papers and waiting to hear the 7 o'clock news on the radio, when the 'phone rang. I reached out and grabbed the receiver. The voice at the other end belonged to *Daily Express* Picture Editor,

Frank Spooner. He told me that Charlie Wilson had been tracked down and arrested in Canada. At that moment Charlie was being held in a police station in downtown Montreal, while Tommy Butler (also in Canada) anxiously awaited the arrival of extradition papers for Wilson from London.

Frank told me I was booked on the 11 o'clock flight to Montreal. The office knew of my friendship with Charlie and, banking on this knowledge, I believe they expected me to return with a scoop. Within hours I was on board a Boeing-707 flying across the Atlantic.

Sitting there in the first-class compartment, sipping a glass of excellent champagne, I couldn't help reminiscing about the old days in South London. Charlie and I had never been really close, at least not in the way Gordon and I were, but we'd had a lot of laughs and good times together. We had both come a long way since those days, and I wondered at the strange twist of fate that was to bring us together again on the other side of the Atlantic. As the Boeing began its descent I looked out and saw the city of Montreal covered in a blanket of snow.

I took a taxi through the cold streets to the Hotel Boneventure where the *Express* had booked a room for me. As I signed the hotel register, I saw several old acquaintances among the group of correspondents congregating in the lobby. All the New York boys attached to British newspapers were there. Word soon got around that I knew some of the Great Train Robbers and for a while, as they pumped me with questions about my association with Charlie, I became the centre of attention.

I quickly caught up with the story-so-far. Charlie had been living a normal, conventional life with his family in the suburb of Rigaud and had been arrested while taking his children to school.

The police were being difficult, refusing to give away much information on the situation. Several of my colleagues had tried, unsuccessfully, to make contact with Charlie's wife, Pat. I reasoned that I had the edge in this particular department, for although we had never met I assumed Pat would know about me through Charlie. With this in mind, I drove out to Charlie's home, almost 30 miles outside the city.

Unlike the neighbouring houses, no one had found time to clear the snow from the path leading to the Wilsons' front-door. A wisp of smoke rose from the thin chimney of the central heating system, a poignant reminder of the ordinary, everyday life Charlie and his family had been living, a life that had been shattered just a few hours earlier.

I rang the doorbell, but there was no reply. I waited a while longer, kicking my feet against the door-step in an effort to keep warm. There was still no answer. I was about to leave when a couple came out of a house nearby and I asked them if they knew where Pat Wilson could be found. They told me she had gone into hiding but they didn't know where. They also told me how shocked they had been to learn of their neighbour's true identity on the radio news bulletins that morning. The Wilsons had always been model neighbours, always courteous and polite, and had fitted comfortably into the Rigaud way of life. I thanked the couple and walked back to the car.

Back at the Hotel Boneventure I telephoned Charlie's lawyers. I explained my past association with their celebrated client and asked if I might speak with him. This was not possible, but I was able to talk to Pat for a while. She was due to see Charlie later that day and promised to tell him that I had flown from London to cover his return to Britain. I also managed to track down some close friends of the family, but they were too loyal to divulge any information about Charlie's whereabouts, and were too involved, anyway, in efforts to extricate him from Tommy Butler's firm grip to be able to talk to me for any length of time.

Meanwhile, back at the police station, the long-awaited extradition papers had arrived from London.

Charlie's lawyers made a last-ditch attempt to stop the proceedings, on some technical point of law, but only managed to delay the inevitable by half an hour or so.

The reporters had managed to get some sort of story, but I was still pictureless and becoming more and more frustrated by the minute. None of us knew when Charlie would be flown home. We were working blind, save for a few scraps of information grudgingly supplied by the authorities. Then, one of our contacts on the local press heard that Charlie would be put on the night flight to London, and it was this tit-bit which sent us racing to the airport. We all took a gamble and booked on the same flight.

More nail-biting minutes followed as take-off time approached and still there was no sign of Charlie. I had visions of calling Frank Spooner from London airport and explaining how I'd got on the wrong plane! We were about to battle our way off the plane when we heard a lot of commotion at the rear. Then a smiling steward told us to calm down as Charlie had been brought on board at the last minute. Soon we were bound for London.

I began to relax and plan the next move in the game. Luck was on my side, since I was the only photographer on the plane. With the approval of my colleagues I sent a note to Charlie, via Tommy Butler, asking if he would see me for a few moments. Butler's reply came quickly: 'No.' Charlie Wilson would see no one.

That, I decided, was that. There was nothing else I could do, except sit back, drink a few glasses of champagne, try to catch up on my sleep and resign myself to the fact that I had tried my best. Yet, at the same time, I had the kind of premonition I've had on many stories. I felt that I only had to play it cool and something would happen to enable me to get my scoop picture.

Sure enough, two hours later, a stewardess approached me. 'Are you Terry Fincher?' she asked. I said 'Yes', and she told me to go to the back of the plane, unaccompanied. Charlie had asked to see me.

Premonition or not, I could hardly believe my luck and nor could my colleagues. They looked enviously up from their card games and drinks. Fortunately, Ian Brodie, a *Daily Express* foreign correspondent, was also on board and he helped to persuade them to allow me to make contact with Charlie. If I didn't, he argued, the whole story could be lost for all of us. I gave my word not to ruin the story for them and continued to the back of the plane.

Charlie was in a window seat and handcuffed to Tommy Butler. Next to Butler sat a detective-sergeant. The strain of the past two days showed on the faces of all three men. The detective-sergeant moved from his seat to let me sit down but I still had to lean across Tommy Butler to speak to Charlie.

'Hello, mate,' said Charlie. 'Pat told me you were around.'

We talked of the old days for a while and Butler told us to keep our voices down. Charlie laughed at the whole ridiculous situation. 'What a way to meet again!' he exclaimed. 'Half-way across the Atlantic, and me chained to a copper!'

Finally, I asked, 'Can I take your picture, Charlie?'

'You'd better ask the Guv'nor,' he said, indicating Butler with an unexpected measure of respect.

Tommy Butler agreed reluctantly. I believe he sensed it would be an historic picture or, at least, certainly one for his scrapbook.

Then it was Charlie's turn to be awkward. 'I want £30,000 for my story, Terry,' he said. 'I need the money.'

Butler bristled. 'Don't talk about that sort of thing in front of me!' he said. But he was, at heart, a kind man and he knew what Charlie had just said to be perfectly true. He knew that, like most runaway Great Train Robbers, Charlie would have blown most of his takings on expensive escape-routes and laying false trails. Butler must also have seen the looks on the faces of Charlie's children when the arrest had been made and knew that Pat would need all the help she could get in bringing them up. Obligingly, he turned a deaf ear to the rest of our conversation.

I was in no position to authorize a payment of the size Charlie had asked for, so I made the best offer I could.

'All I can offer on my own is £200. I know it's not much, Charlie. But I promise to speak to my Editor, I'm sure he'll want to make an offer for your story. It's the best I can do, mate.'

Charlie turned his head to look out at the night, then turned back to me. 'Okay, Terry. You can have your picture. I know I can trust you.' He then wrote me a note, authorizing the sale of his story for £30,000.

There was very little light inside the compartment, so I brought out a flash-gun and began attaching it to my camera.

'You can't do that,' warned Tommy Butler.

'What?' I asked.

'You can't use flash.'

'Why not?'

'You must consider the other passengers,' said Butler. 'They don't know what's going on and I don't want you attracting any attention to us.'

It was still night-time over the Atlantic and the cabin lights were far too dim for photography, so I would have to wait until dawn for my picture. More frustration.

I arranged with Tommy Butler for my colleagues to be allowed back for a brief interview with Charlie, then I went forward again.

I explained the situation to Ian Brodie who realized that, with the pictures I hoped to take and the extra copy he would get from my chat with Charlie, the scoop would be almost 'in the bag'. Then we explained the deal to our companions. They could speak with Charlie, provided I got exclusive pictures (I had since learned that one of the reporters was carrying a camera). They considered the proposal for a while and finally had to agree to it.

After what seemed the longest night of my life, the cabin began to fill with pale morning light. I picked up my camera-bag and crept past my sleeping colleagues on my way back to see Charlie.

Using a 35-mm Leica with a wide-angle lens I made just six exposures at ⅛th second; it seemed a hell of a long way to go for just a few shots at that shutter speed and I knew I would be sweating with nervousness

all the way to the darkroom. Afterwards I thanked Charlie and Tommy Butler, then returned to my seat.

Even though my pictures were in the bag I still had to protect them, and when Ian and I learned that a crowd of photographers and TV newsmen were waiting to join the plane at Prestwick we realized we had to kill any further coverage. Quickly I went back to explain the situation to Charlie. He agreed to keep out of sight on the last leg of the flight from Prestwick to Heathrow. Tommy Butler couldn't see what all the fuss was about, but he moved Charlie to a forward compartment.

The flight between Prestwick and Heathrow was quite a comedy, the intrepid cameramen trying to climb over the seats to get at Charlie, and airline officials trying to hold them back. But Charlie was true to his word and remained hidden from view.

The Boeing finally touched down at Heathrow. The pressmen who had boarded in Scotland were cleared first, along with other passengers. Then Tommy Butler and Charlie Wilson prepared to leave. Charlie kissed the stewardess good-bye and thanked her for all her help.

'See you, Terry,' he said and we shook hands. Then he covered his head with an overcoat and descended the steps of the plane.

He was met by the largest battery of journalists I'd seen for years: the sort of reception that used to be reserved for Royalty or visiting Heads of State. I followed him down the steps and watched as he was bustled away through the crowd by Tommy Butler and several burly policemen. They shoved him into a waiting car and whisked him away from the scene.

Within the hour I was back at the *Daily Express* building in Fleet Street, anxiously awaiting the results from the darkroom. I had mixed feelings when I saw the pictures. Professionally speaking I knew I had a great scoop, and it was another story finished. But emotionally I was choked-up inside. It might

Overleaf
Charlie Wilson (left) handcuffed to Tommy Butler en route for London, 28 January 1968

have been over for me, but for Charlie it was just beginning, and he was soon to be safely locked away.

I arrived home on Sunday evening. Frank Spooner telephoned and told me to return to Montreal next day to negotiate with Pat Wilson for the sale of her story of life 'on the run' with Charlie.

My first-light picture of Charlie Wilson handcuffed to his captor, Tommy Butler, appeared on the front page of Monday's edition. I received a bonus for my part in the scoop, but somehow it seemed a rather sad way to get it and the world seemed a bloody strange place as I read and re-read that story on the flight back to Canada.

As it happened, another newspaper obtained the story, but it was some comfort to know that Charlie's family finally got some of the security he had asked for.

I received several Christmas cards from Charlie while he was in prison and I once photographed some of the pictures he painted there. He was released in 1978 but I've not heard from him since.

While covering the Royal tour by Prince Charles to South America in 1978, I met another Great Train Robber, perhaps the most famous of them all – Ronnie Biggs.

Biggs's dramatic flight to Brazil, via Australia, is now part of English criminal history. When I met him he had recently made a record with the Sex Pistols and its imminent release was gaining much space in the Press back home. I travelled with an ITN film crew to his home, a large detached house in the tiny fishing village of Courea Nues – some forty miles from Rio de Janeiro

Ronnie Biggs with his son, Mike, Brazil, 1978

– where he was living with his young son, Mike.

'I accept what has happened to me,' he said. 'But I've got no regrets. I would love to go back home. Give myself up. But by the time I got out again I'd be an old man . . . .'

I often think back to that thin wisp of smoke rising from Charlie Wilson's empty house in Rigaud, and I'm filled with sadness for him, for Goody, and for Biggs. For them, it was all such a waste of time.

Gordon Goody once said to me: 'If you didn't have a job like yours, Terry, you'd have been one of the boys.' Personally I doubt it, but thankfully I'll never know if he was right or not.

5

Royalty

My first assignment upon rejoining Keystone as a full-time professional in 1951 had been to cover the planting of a tree in Kensington Gardens by the Princess Royal. I was the only photographer to turn up on that gloomy November afternoon and it turned out be one of my least-inspired jobs. I exposed three slides on my 9 × 12 plate camera and was soon on board a No. 9 bus on the way back to Fleet Street, feeling little confidence in the pictures I had taken (none of which, incidentally, ever saw the light of day in any newspaper). Little did I dream, on that journey back to the Keystone office, that in years to come I would be travelling the world to photograph the Royal family, and on several occasions meeting them personally.

One evening just before Christmas that same year I stood outside Buckingham Palace waiting to snatch a car-picture of the King and Queen as they drove out of the gates at the start of their journey to Sandringham where they were to spend the holidays. Assignments like this were the old hardy chestnuts which press photographers would cover without fail every season and over the next few years I would find myself out in all weathers photographing the merest

movements of the Royal family. I always considered this particular area of the job as being a bit like game shooting – most of the time it was more a matter of luck than judgement whether you got your picture or not. Even if you were fortunate enough to spot a Royal personage glancing your way, the chances were that the old type of flashbulb wouldn't synchronize with the camera shutter and the moment would be lost for ever. The picture I attempted that evening didn't turn out and was sadly to prove my last opportunity to photograph King George VI. This immensely popular monarch died at Sandringham on 6 February 1952.

That day I was working on a story at the Blue Cross animal clinic in Fulham. Midge telephoned me there and, amid the noise of the animals, I listened as he told me the news of the King's death. I passed on the news to other people in the clinic and watched the expressions of utter disbelief appear on their faces as they repeated the words 'The King is dead.' Midge then ordered me back to the office where I would be put on standby to cover further developments.

The body of King George VI was brought back from Sandringham to lie in state inside

Westminster Hall. Thousands of loyal subjects lined the route as the procession bearing his coffin made its way through the streets of London. I had been allocated a position, which I shared with another photographer, on a rooftop overlooking Trafalgar Square. We stood on a plank of rotting wood previously used by fire-watchers during the war. As the procession approached we both leaned forward for a better view. Suddenly the plank broke and we slid together down the greasy tiles, with only the rain-guttering saving us from falling onto the crowd below. I recovered quickly and got my pictures before making the precarious climb back to safety.

Next day I picked up my cameras, slipped a dozen slides into my pocket and caught a bus to Westminster. The scene outside the entrance to Westminster Hall was astonishing. The line of people waiting to pay their last respects to the King stretched right along the embankment and over Lambeth Bridge. I walked along the silent line, photographing particularly poignant expressions. Yet no one seemed to mind my presence, for they were all preoccupied with their grief. I quickly used up all my slides and returned to Fleet Street. All three evening papers used my pictures that night, as did most of the national dailies next morning.

It was a custom at Keystone that any photographer who had more than six publications of any one photograph on the same day won a guinea, and, by way of celebration, had to buy tea for all the other photographers. The following morning Midge greeted me as I entered the office. He had a big smile on his face. 'You've got a guinea, lad. Put it on your expenses,' he said. But despite my success I felt miserable for earning it on such a sad occasion.

On 23 June 1953, I covered Queen Elizabeth II's Coronation procession from what must have been the least glamorous position of the day – the roof of the gents' toilet at Hyde Park Corner.

I had slept overnight in the Keystone office as I had to be in position by 6.30 in the morning. (Why, I still don't know, since the Coronation Coach would not be passing my perch until about three o'clock in the afternoon.)

It was pouring with rain when I awoke that morning and I was about to leave the office when Arthur Marsh, arriving early for a busy day in the despatch department, noticed I had no coat (because I simply couldn't afford one). 'Better take mine,' he said sympathetically. He handed me the smart, dark-blue, gaberdine raincoat which had served him well since his demobilization from the Navy. 'And bloody well look after it,' he said as I thanked him.

The downpour continued all morning and by midday I was a very soggy specimen atop that toilet. The rain ran continuously down my neck, my shirt was drenched and, to make matters worse, Arthur's coat had begun to disintegrate on my back.

Eventually the procession passed by, with Queen Salote of Tonga – a tall, elegant lady wearing a bright red feather in her hat – completely winning the heart of the crowd by her refusal to have the hood of her coach up against the rain. But even Queen Salote was overshadowed by the arrival of the newly crowned Queen Elizabeth II. I'll never forget the view through my camera as she passed by in that splendid golden coach.

Back at the office I handed in my plates, then returned Arthur's coat to him. He was convinced that I had fallen into the Serpentine and he never wore that coat again for the simple reason that it was unwearable.

During the final years of the 1950s I spent a great deal of time photographing the Royal family in Britain. I photographed the Royal children growing up, going to school, going on holiday. One Christmas I snapped Prince Charles and Princess Anne enjoying all the fun of the fair as they rode the dodgems while on a trip to Bertram Mills's Circus at Olympia.

I took what is perhaps my most daring Royal picture around this time. The occasion was Princess Margaret's visit to the Isle

Princess Margaret, Isle of Sark, late 1950s

of Sark. All motor vehicles are prohibited on this tiny island, which meant we had to cover the event on foot.

One day after chasing the Princess's horse-drawn carriage all the way up a very steep hill, we eventually caught up with her as she stepped down to view the scene from the hilltop. She was dressed in the fashion of the day, a very tight skirt, and looked very attractive as she gazed out over the island. I happened to be on the opposite side of the carriage when the Princess climbed back into it. Inevitably her skirt rode up to reveal stocking-tops and suspenders, also the fash-

ion of the day. Naturally, I took the picture.

Later I wired the photograph back to the *Daily Herald*. Almost immediately I received a call from Len Hickman. He told me that the paper thought the shot was too 'sexy' and that he had 'killed' it. He also ordered me to destroy all my prints. I did – all except one!

On a snowy day in January 1960 the wedding of David Hicks and Lady Pamela Mountbatten took place at Romsey Abbey in Hampshire. Princess Anne was a bridesmaid and I

'Snow Princess', 1960

'Farewell Edwina': the funeral of Lady Mountbatten, HMS *Wakeful,* 1960

took a picture of her as she was framed charmingly by a snow-covered car window. After the ceremony a reception was held for the workers at Broadlands, the Mountbatten estate nearby. The Royal family stood on the stage of the small hall and watched as the bride and groom cut the cake. It was a happy occasion. I remember that, at one point, Lady Mountbatten approached me to ask if I had taken any nice photographs.

Six weeks later tragedy struck the Mountbatten family. Lady Mountbatten died in Borneo while on a tour of the Far East and her body was brought back to England.

On a grey, misty day in February I sailed from Portsmouth harbour in a Royal Navy escort vessel to cover the funeral which, as Lady Edwina had wished, took place at sea. The ceremony was performed by the Archbishop of Canterbury on board HMS *Wakeful*, berthed four miles south of Nab Tower on the Isle of Wight.

I photographed the funeral from the bridge of the escort vessel a few hundred yards from the *Wakeful*. Using a 500-mm lens, I focused on the mourners grouped around the coffin draped in a Union Jack. Among those accompanying Lord Mountbatten were Prince Philip and Princess Alice of Greece. It was difficult to keep the ceremony within my viewfinder as the boat rocked up and down, but what I did see appeared rather like a solemn, silent film. When Lady Mountbatten's coffin slipped beneath the grey waters, her husband picked up a wreath of lilies and kissed the flowers before casting it onto the sea. I captured the moment and next day my picture appeared in the *Daily Herald* headlined 'Farewell Edwina'.

Also in 1960, Princess Margaret announced her engagement to Antony Armstrong-Jones, a well-known photographer. His work had appeared occasionally in the *Daily Express* and other Fleet Street journals yet, in the street that's supposed to know it all, no one had so much as an inkling of the romance. The couple had

met when he was commissioned to photograph the Royal children; they had managed to keep their relationship a secret for two years and now their wedding was to take place in Westminster Abbey on 6 May.

At that time my only encounter with the bridegroom-to-be had been a society wedding in Mayfair. There had been the usual large mob of photographers pushing and shoving in the confined entrance to the church, awaiting the arrival of Sir Winston. Tony's Leica was damaged in the crush and he turned to ask my advice. 'Sorry, I don't know anything about Leicas,' I said impatiently. I had never used a Leica before and was trying to concentrate on the job in hand. I had no time to worry about someone else's damaged equipment and he probably thought me rude and unhelpful.

I covered the wedding of Antony Armstrong-Jones and Princess Margaret (as one of the official pool of photographers) from my allocated position high up on a plat-

Lord Snowdon and Lucy Lindsay-Hogg after their wedding at Kensington Register Office

Royal Wedding, Westminster Abbey, 6 May 1960

form between the pillars in the Abbey. Once again I was up in the air, although this was a bit different from the roofing in Trafalgar Square and a lot drier than it had been on top of the gents' toilet at Hyde Park Corner. But even this exalted position was not without its problems too. As I climbed down from the platform after the ceremony, the tails of my Moss Bros morning suit got caught up in the scaffolding, and several precious minutes passed before I was able to free myself and get my urgent film away.

Perhaps the most memorable tour of recent years was the visit made by the Queen and Prince Philip to India, Pakistan, Nepal and Iran in 1961. For me, the honour of being selected as one of the three Fleet Street photographers who would cover this tour was marred by a personal tragedy. My mother was taken ill a week or so before I was due to depart. I visited her in hospital and felt reluctant to go on the tour knowing she was unwell. As always, she sensed my inner feelings, and realizing the importance of such an opportunity, settled the matter once and for all by insisting that I go. She asked me, in her soft Irish accent, to bring back some jade for her, and she promised to be up and about again by the time I got back. As I said good-bye to her I had no idea that she had cancer. She knew it herself, but insisted that it be kept secret from me until my return.

The tour was to be my first visit to India. I travelled with *Daily Herald* writer Anthony Carthew in advance of the Royal party to help produce some curtain-raising stories prior to their arrival. We flew out of London in the depths of winter and landed in Delhi at the height of an Indian summer.

I can remember the moment I first set foot in India. It was an unforgettable experience. The orange glow of dawn was fading into daylight and the heady smell of the place hit me as soon as the door of our Comet opened at Delhi airport. Since then I have visited India several times and have come to know it as perhaps the most fascinating country of them all.

As Anthony and I drove through the streets of the city in a ramshackle taxi we passed many plodding ox-carts and hundreds of people scurrying to work. We passed a newly built luxury hotel and, just a mile or so further on, the poverty-stricken streets of the homeless.

Anthony summed it up best when he later wrote: 'Where else on earth do you feel so powerless to do anything as your stomach jerks at the sights. India makes the Middle East look like a welfare state. And yet . . . so much has been done. Hundreds of schools have been built . . factories are rearing up . . . .'

He went on: 'These are the contrasts of India: jasmine and lepers, 20-course meals and a bowl of rice to last a week, temples and hovels, stench and perfume, silks and rags, beauty and sores, squalor and greatness, disease and glory. This is the terrible and marvellous atmosphere of India.'

The tour took us the length and breadth of the land – from the snow-covered Himalayas

The Queen with Prime Minister Nehru, India, 1961

Princess Anne and friends on holiday in France, early 1960s

60

to the tropical gardens in Madras. In Bombay – the Gateway to India – the Royal couple met Indians who seemed more English than we were, an echo of the distant days of the Raj. In Agra they visited the Taj Mahal where I photographed them gazing down at their reflections in an ornamental pool. In Jaipur the Queen entered the city on the back of a beautifully decorated elephant. We moved on to Calcutta, another hot and steamy city crammed with countless people living in desperate poverty and suffering. There, the Queen rode for the first time in an open-topped limousine and stood waving to the thousands who had turned out to greet her. People were clinging to trees; they were perched on roof-tops; they stood on cars or anything else which would give them a glimpse of Her Majesty.

On a Royal rest day in Bengal, the Duke of Edinburgh went on a tiger-shoot. Rest days are private and the accompanying Press kept well away. However, stories do leak out and on this particular occasion so did a picture taken, I believe, by a privileged friend. The picture showed a large tiger lying dead as a doornail at the feet of the Duke and others. It was a harmless holiday memento, until it appeared next day in several English newspapers. A flood of protest followed from animal lovers and preservationists all over the country. How, they wondered, could Prince Philip reconcile the fact of hunting wild-life while at the same time campaigning for its preservation? It was all very embarrassing for the Duke, even more so as he was scheduled to go on another tiger-shoot in a few days' time with King Mahendra in Nepal. A solution had to be found which would please everybody.

In Kathmandu, the capital of Nepal, the band struck up 'God Save The Queen' and King Mahendra stepped forward to greet the Royal couple. It was then we noticed that the Duke's right arm was in a sling and that his index finger was heavily bandaged. 'That's his bloody trigger-finger!' remarked a nearby reporter.

The Duke wore a satisfied smile on his face and we were told he had a painful whitlow on his finger. The Royal party did go out

to shoot tigers, but only with cameras. Thus diplomacy was observed in Nepal and further controversy avoided in Britain.

In Tehran, as the tour drew towards its end, I received a call from June. She told me that my mother was dying. I caught the next flight home.

My mother, having discharged herself from hospital, was lying in the front room of her Putney home. I gave her a present – the jade she had asked for. I held her hand and told her of the great things I had seen in India. She died a few days later and all my adventures of the previous weeks were forgotten in my grief. We had always been very close. She had encouraged my interest in photography; she had loaned me money to buy equipment, and had followed my career with pride. Now she was gone.

I think it is true to say that my mother's death brought my father and me a little closer. From that day on I believe I began to understand him better than I had done in the past.

Despite protestations from the government, the Queen and Prince Philip were determined to go on their scheduled tour of Commonwealth countries in West Africa in November 1961. The government's concern stemmed from the fact that a bomb had exploded near President Nkrumah's statue in Accra, capital of Ghana, just a few days before the Royal Party's planned departure. I was in Accra to cover the preparations for the tour and had witnessed the panic the bombing had caused so I, too, wondered if it was safe for the Queen to enter such a trouble-torn region.

Commonwealth Secretary Duncan Sandys immediately flew out to Ghana to travel along some of the routes the Queen would be taking, setting himself up as a target and making sure it was safe for her. He must have decided that all was well, since the Royal couple arrived on time and the tour began as scheduled.

However, all was not necessarily well for

The Queen and Prince Philip confer as they watch 'Su-Su' dancers on tour of West Africa, 1961

us, the members of the British Press in Ghana. Some people there had taken exception to Fleet Street's reporting of the bomb incident and the atmosphere was tense, to say the least. One evening I was having a quiet drink in the bar of our hotel when several angry Ghanaians rushed up to a nearby table and accused two of my colleagues of having no respect for Ghana, as they had not stood up for the National Anthem. The situation was serious and carried the threat of arrest. Fortunately the tension passed when we explained that the Anthem had been played more than a hundred yards away at the other end of the hotel and had been virtually indistinguishable at that distance from an earlier rendition of Glenn Miller's 'In the Mood'.

It is a rule always observed on Royal tours that no accompanying aircraft may take off until forty minutes after the Royal flight has been cleared. One evening when she had completed her engagements in a remote village up-country in Ghana, the Queen took off an hour before dusk heading for Accra. Half an hour later, the old twin-engined Dakota carrying the Press party lifted into the rapidly darkening sky and we soon ran into a heavy thunderstorm. We couldn't return to the up-country airstrip as it possessed no landing lights. There was no way around the storm and our small aircraft would not climb above it, so it was a matter of ploughing straight on. The Dakota was thrown from side to side with lightning continuously reflecting on the wings. I sat by the rear door with my good friend Mike McKeown, a *Daily Express* photographer. Mike is a devout Catholic and he said several 'Hail Mary's' while using his sleeve to keep the rain from entering through a crack in the door. It came as a great relief when we eventually bumped down in Accra.

In Gambia, our Press party were scheduled to follow the Royal party up the river Gambia in a specially chartered boat. It was to be an overnight trip from Bathurst, arriving at a remote village early the next morning.

Mike and I were shown to a small, filthy cabin which had a large hole in the floor, a closer inspection revealing it to be a rat-hole complete with teeth marks where the animal had gnawed its way in. We dumped our bags on our bunks and I blocked up the hole with several layers of cardboard torn from my sandwich box. We tried to settle in the cabin but it was too depressing so we eventually spent the night in deck-chairs up top. Most of our fellow-travellers had made the same decision. We joined in a card-school on deck and settled down for a game of poker under a starry sky. We had played just a couple of hands when we heard a splash in the water, followed by a loud scream. We rushed to the rails to see what had happened: 'Some poor bugger's fallen in, darling,' said Annie Lloyd-Williams, a *Daily Mirror* reporter. 'He fell off the gangway as he was coming on board.'

Someone else said it was a local native carrying luggage on board. The seconds passed in silence as people squinted down into the water, but there was no sign, or sound, of life in the water.

A crew member's voice split the silence. 'He stands no chance, the crocs will have him by now,' he said almost nonchalantly.

Soon the missing man's wife and children stood on the dockside screaming and crying and we felt completely helpless as we listened to them. A Royal Navy boat from one of *Britannia*'s escort vessels made a fruitless search. There was nothing anyone could do.

Eventually we untied and began our journey up the river Gambia. The old boat was listing badly to starboard but the Captain, who looked and sounded like Paul Robeson, assured us it was all right. 'Just a faulty pump.'

By now Mike and I, like most others on board, felt miserable and in need of a stiff drink. We both went below with the intention of knocking back the half bottle of Scotch we had brought for the trip. To our amazement a large rat was sitting on the table nibbling at my sandwiches. He had eaten his way through the cardboard I'd stuffed in the hole in the cabin and took little notice as Mike grabbed the bottle. Leaving the rat to enjoy my sandwiches we hurried back up to the deck.

Royal safety was feared for once again on the tour of Canada in October 1964. The French Separatist movement was in full swing in Quebec, and their anti-monarchist views were widely known. The Royal couple were advised to travel in a bullet-proof car. Extra police were called in to control the vast crowds expected to turn out. However, in anticipation of violence the citizens of Quebec stayed well away and I photographed the Royal motorcade driving through nearly deserted streets, flanked by hundreds of policemen and Royal Canadian mounties.

On this tour I shared the company of two of the all-time greats of British journalism, foreign correspondents Vincent Mulchrone of the *Daily Mail* and René McColl, with whom I was covering the tour for the *Daily Express*. One evening Vincent and I were enjoying a bottle of champagne and some delicious Prince Edward Island oysters in the hotel bar when I spotted René's face reflected in the mirror behind the bar. He was frantically beckoning me to come outside without attracting Vincent's attention.

I excused myself from the bar and nonchalantly walked out into the street where René was waiting. 'Get your camera, quickly!' he said excitedly, while checking through the window that Vincent's suspicions had not been roused by my sudden departure.

It was not until we were seated in a speeding taxi that René explained what was going on. He had heard about a Separatist meeting being held in a downtown theatre and he felt that 'these bloody French fanatics' might make a good story.

Although I speak very little French I soon got the gist of the meeting. They objected to the Queen's presence in Quebec and, judging from René's agitated reactions, they were saying some pretty nasty things about her. Suddenly René leapt to his feet, shouting: 'Bloody traitors, you should all be hanged!'

In seconds we were surrounded by an angry mob who were so close I couldn't raise my camera to take a photograph. Luckily there were several policemen around

and, with revolvers, they escorted René and me from the theatre and into another taxi. Back at the hotel René rushed off to the telex-room to send the story of the angry mob and their insult to the Queen back to the *Express*.

Less than half an hour had passed since I had left Vincent at the bar. When I rejoined him he asked me where I'd been. I told him the story. 'Christ! If there's no news about, René will find some.' Next day René received a congratulatory cable from the Editor.

René and I moved on to New York where he was to write some 'special features' on the USA and where I was to stand in for Bill Lovelace, the *Daily Express* photographer based in America, who had flown back to London to be with his pregnant wife. Other newspapermen who had been with us in Canada went on their way to Mexico to report on the visit there by Prince Philip.

This was my first trip to the States and I was really looking forward to working there. However, we had barely had time to unpack before we were instructed to arrange the necessary accreditation to fly to Moscow where the news of Khrushchev's dismissal from office had just broken. Personally, I was disappointed by these orders as I much preferred the promise of freedom in New York to the prospect of restrictions in Moscow. Luckily, the Russian Embassy in Washington refused to grant either of us the necessary visas. But back at the *Express* office a new set of instructions awaited me – I was to go to Mexico, after all, and team up with *Daily Express* reporter Donald Seamen. So, within hours of leaving them I was reunited with my colleagues from the Canadian tour.

Freddie Reed of the *Daily Mirror*, one of the most charming and courteous of all Fleet Street photographers, informed me that our best opportunity for good pictures would occur on the Duke's visit to the *hacienda* of a prominent rancher. The *hacienda* was a splendid building set in the middle of real cowboy country, some 80 miles from Mexico City. In the centre of its cobbled courtyard stood a pleasant fountain surrounded

64

by flowers, and giving the impression that it was actually cooling the air. Distinguished-looking men dressed in traditional Mexican attire strolled around while their horses were being prepared with elaborately decorated bridles and saddles. To complete the scene a *Mariachi* band was playing in the background – a perfect setting under a cloudless blue sky.

The only discordant note was unwittingly struck by the Royal visitor himself. Prince Philip was ushered into the house and emerged a short while later, looking distinctly uncomfortable in a tight-fitting Mexican outfit complete with sombrero, cowboy-style chaps, high-heeled boots and a pair of six-guns slung at his sides in leather holsters.

We asked if we might take some photographs.

'Get a bloody move on, then,' said the Duke sharply. We took a few shots, then the distinguished bunch quickly mounted up, rode off at a fair turn of speed and were soon gone in a cloud of dust.

Freddie and I were beginning to feel the effects of the hot sun and so stood little chance of following the party. We sat together in a shaded spot and had just begun to bemoan the fact that we had come all this way for a few pictures, when a local lad came up to us. He told us, in broken English, that he knew a short-cut to the place where the party were headed. We followed him along a path through tall cactus plants, eventually arriving at a near-deserted village, complete with lopsided church. The windows of all the houses were shuttered and the only sign of life came from a couple of scrawny chickens scratching in the dirt.

I asked our young friend if anyone lived in the village. 'Si, señor,' he said and awkwardly explained that the entire population had gone to join the celebrations in honour of the Duke, in the next village. But, he assured us with a grin, Prince Philip would pass our way on his return to the *hacienda*.

An hour or so later Freddie and I had begun seriously to doubt our young friend's information, especially as he had climbed well out of our reach, up to the top of a tall

cactus. But suddenly he was laughing and pointing to a cloud of dust on the horizon. 'Banditos,' he called out, giggling as the cloud drew nearer.

The Duke of Edinburgh was riding ahead of his distinguished hosts and looking more like John Wayne than a Royal Prince. He posed for us with other members of his party in front of the crooked-looking church and he seemed to be enjoying himself, at last.

We rewarded our young friend and returned to the *hacienda*, hot and tired, but happy in the knowledge that our long trek had finally been worth while.

In January 1965 I was sent with the Royal tour to Ethiopia and the Sudan (on which the Queen and Prince Philip were scheduled to meet Emperor Haile Selassie in Addis Ababa). Before their arrival the *Daily Express* African correspondent, John Monks, arranged a private audience for himself and me, with the Emperor.

We arrived at the Palace and were told to

Prince Philip in Mexican attire, 1964

The Queen and Emperor Haile Selassie at the Tississat Falls

wait at the gate, where sat one of the Emperor's pet lions tied on a short lead. Needing a good shot to illustrate John's article I stepped forward to photograph the lion. The beast leapt at me and was within licking distance of my lens before I had a chance to press the shutter. I fell back in terror, realizing I'd underestimated the length of the lead. I damaged one of my cameras in the process and was still in a state of shock when John and I stood before the tiny Emperor's desk.

My fright had been worth it, though, for a few days later I photographed the Queen and Haile Selassie looking out over the Tississat Falls at the source of the Nile, a picture which was spread over five columns in the following day's *Daily Express*.

In the spring of 1965, I found myself in something of a dilemma. On 25 March, the Duke of Windsor, formerly King Edward VIII, had returned to London to undergo an eye operation. He was staying with his wife the Duchess, formerly Mrs Wallis Simpson, at Claridge's Hotel. I was assigned to 'door-step' them.

One afternoon I was talking outside the hotel with *Paris Match* photographer Roy Dickens, when the Duke's grey-and-black Rolls Royce pulled up at the kerb. Moments later the Duke and Duchess left the hotel and climbed into the car. Roy and I immediately hailed a passing taxi and delivered the classic line: 'Follow that car!'

We followed 'that car' to the inner circle of Regent's Park where it pulled up near St Mary's Garden, named for the Duke's mother. Roy and I took several shots as the Duke was helped from the car by a Special Branch detective, then he spotted our cameras and called us over to him. The Duke shook my hand and requested us not to follow him into the garden nor to take any more photographs as he still felt under the weather following the operation and was not looking his best. Reluctantly we agreed, and shuffled our feet by the gate as the Duke, the

Duchess and the detective disappeared behind the small hill.

Soon, however, curiosity began to get the better of us and we found a small gap in the hedge through which we could see them strolling among the spring flowers. Here was one of the most famous couples in the world whose romance had once made headline news everywhere. The temptation was too great. I quickly attached a 500-mm lens to my camera and took several shots. Roy and I waited out of sight until the distinguished couple had departed, then I made my way back to Fleet Street.

I was torn between my obligations. I had given my word to the Duke to take no more photographs, yet I knew I had a good picture worthy of publication. A print of the best shot was made while I explained the situation to *Daily Express* Editor, Derek Marks. He agreed that since I'd given my word, we couldn't publish. But when he saw

I meet the Duke of Windsor in Regent's Park, March, 1965

The Duke and Duchess of Windsor, accompanied by a detective, stroll in Queen Mary's Garden, Regent's Park, March 1965. Published as a half page in the following day's *Daily Express*

the pictures he decided to send a complimentary print to the Duke and Duchess, explaining our predicament and asking their permission to publish after all.

Fortunately, they thought it a charming picture and consented to its publication and at the same time ordered more copies for the Duke and Duchess.

There have been many Royal assignments since then, but perhaps the most enjoyable was the visit made by Prince Charles to Brazil and Venezuela in 1978.

On the second evening of the tour Prince Charles witnessed one of Brazil's national institutions, a demonstration of the Samba. He began by watching from a balcony overlooking the dance floor on which several

very beautiful girls in glamorous and revealing costumes swayed to the heady beat of the music, their near-naked bodies glistening in the warm evening air. Trumpets and whistles were blowing away in the background and the Prince was soon caught up in the infectious atmosphere. He came down and began dancing with a luscious-looking lady who wore no more than a layer of feathers. It was like the Charge of the Light Brigade as we clambered towards him; everyone was pushing and shoving. I was grabbed by a very tall, big-bosomed lady with hundreds of feathers protruding from her costume, and for what seemed an eternity I was lost in the frenzied movements of her plumage. When I managed to surface again I had the good fortune to find myself directly in front of the Prince who was still dancing with his dusky

Prince Charles dances the Samba, Rio de Janeiro, 1978

68

partner. I shot off two pictures before my feathered friend smothered me again.

The tour moved north to Manaus, a hot, sticky town on the upper reaches of the Amazon. One evening fellow photographer Serge Lemoine and I were joined for a drink by Lord Snowdon, formerly Antony Armstrong-Jones, who was there on a tough assignment. In the course of conversation he explained that even though it would be a simple matter for him to trade on his famous name to get preferential treatment, he refused to do so. I found him modest and unassuming and expecting no special favours. I respect him for this and I respect his photography, too, for this quiet, kindly man is a gifted photographer. (Later in the year Snowdon married for the second time. His bride was Lucy Lindsay-Hogg, a film researcher. Their wedding took place in the Kensington Register Office and this time I stood on a step-ladder in the pouring rain to record the event. It was a far cry for both of us from the pomp and splendour of his first wedding.)

In Venezuela, after spending a week-end camping at the famous Angel Falls (where Sir Arthur Conan Doyle is said to have had the inspiration for his book *The Lost World*) Prince Charles was scheduled for a very brief stop at a British-owned mine one hour's flight away. We were to follow him there as the event would obviously command a lot of interest back home. Unfortunately our flight was delayed, mainly by matters of protocol, and as time ticked by we realized that the visit would be over by the time we reached the mine. After much discussion we decided to fly on to the next stop on the tour.

Next morning we were on duty yet again, this time at an aluminium works. The Prince walked towards me wearing a splendidly photogenic safety helmet but, instead of posing as I had expected, he began to question me about the failure to turn up at the mine the previous day. I suspect he had heard of the re-routing of our flight and probably thought we had indulged a little too much in the liquid refreshment on the plane. As I launched into a lengthy explanation about the delay I could hear the clicks and whirrs of my colleagues' cameras behind me and I grew more and more frustrated because I couldn't photograph him in that helmet. But when the future King of England is speaking to you, you can't simply raise your camera and start taking his picture, no matter how good a close-up you might get!

Royal assignments, particularly long tours, are hard work. Even though they are offset by certain privileges and opportunities to witness great spectacles, coupled with the humour of fellow pressmen to brighten up the duller occasions, a photographer must always be on the lookout for those telling, informal moments which are the essence of Royal coverage.

The Archbishop of Canterbury, Robert Runcie, summed it up perfectly when, at the celebrations for the Queen Mother's eightieth birthday on 15 June 1980, he said: 'Royalty puts a human face on the operations of government and provides images with which the people of a nation can identify and which they can love.'

I am happy to say that bringing those images closer to the people has been a very enjoyable part of my career.

6

The Troubled Med

My first foreign assignment came about partly because of a battle fought 12 years earlier. In October 1954 Keystone assigned me to Egypt for the unveiling of the El Alamein Memorial by Field-Marshal Montgomery. I was also to cover the British Trade Fair in Baghdad. The assignment lasted a month and I was given £40 for my expenses. It was my first trip beyond the Isle of Wight.

Diplomatic relations between Egypt and Britain were somewhat strained in 1954 and our landing in Alexandria was greeted by several mean-looking policemen armed with .303 rifles who surrounded the plane, then escorted us through Customs – a disconcerting welcome, to say the least.

The route to El Alamein, which was some 60 miles to the west, was still littered here and there with the debris of the Second World War: old petrol cans, rusty barbed-wire, bomb-craters and shell-holes eroded by the years but still recognizable.

In the British Army Cemetery – where the Memorial had been erected – were row upon row of neat graves, shimmering in the heat-haze. They were the graves of British soldiers killed in the Battle of El Alamein, fought in October 1942, in which Monty's Eighth Army had wrested control of the desert from Rommel's Afrika Korps before pushing on towards Tobruk. Many graves bore the names, ranks and numbers of their occupants while many others were simply marked 'Unknown Soldier'. Just a short distance away lay the German and Italian Army Cemeteries with their own orderly rows and their own unknown soldiers. It was a moving moment when Field-Marshal Montgomery stood in the warm North African sunshine, saluting to the memory of his men.

After the ceremony I travelled to Cairo in the comfort of a Rolls-Royce owned, I believe, by the British Ambassador who was making the same journey, but in the company of Monty. That evening, as I sat in the roof-top restaurant of the Semiramis Hotel with Keystone's Egyptian agent and a representative of the British Embassy, I was beginning to feel important. As the cooling, fragrant breeze blew in across the Nile I told myself that I wasn't doing so bad for a 23-year-old.

A waiter brought the menu and with it came an embarrassing moment. It was printed entirely in French, and I couldn't understand a word! However, I managed to bluff my way through the situation by ordering whatever my companions ordered.

The meal, complemented by a couple of bottles of wine, was delicious and by the time the brandy and cigars arrived I was feeling mellowed and relaxed. By then I had decided that the life of a globe-trotting photographer was definitely the life for me.

'Ah yes,' I thought later, as I lay in my bed staring up at the ceiling, 'this is the life, all right. Plenty of sun, exotic food, good wine and, of course, miles and miles of travel to faraway places with strange-sounding names . . .'

I was brought back to earth next morning when I collected my bill. It totalled £8. This, added to several other expenses already incurred on the trip, knocked a sizeable hole in my original £40, and there were still three and a half weeks to go. Luckily, in Baghdad, I met up with Ron Case, another Keystone photographer. Ron was carrying extra funds and was able to lend me enough cash to last me until the end of the assignment. I continued, with my feet firmly on the ground this time and my hand firmly on my wallet.

Back in London I celebrated my return by taking June dancing at the Hammersmith Palais. I told her all about the things I'd seen; the people running around in what looked like pyjamas or night-shirts; the faces of the women covered by dark veils; young men walking hand-in-hand along chaotic city streets; the 'gilly-gilly men', famous street magicians capable of producing a white mouse from your collar, a cheeping chick from inside your jacket, and half a dozen eggs from your ears! I told her about the belly dance I'd seen in Baghdad, performed in a restaurant-cum-nightclub on the banks of the river Tigris, and of the gun-battle I'd witnessed, from a distance, in trouble-torn Beirut on the way home. My first foreign assignment had been a great adventure and it sowed within me the seeds of a great love of travel which has grown ever since.

During the weeks following my return I began to wonder when and where my next foreign assignment would be. Every so often I found myself thinking back to the El Alamein Memorial and all those graves in the

sun. I tried to imagine what that battle for the desert must have been like and I wondered if I would ever photograph a *real* war.

But there were to be no more trips abroad for me in 1954, or the next year. 1956 seemed to be going the same way – until I was sent to Suez (where I had my 'baptism of fire'). After Suez things remained relatively quiet for a while around the world and the trouble spots seemed few and far between. There were, however, a few notable exceptions of which I was to cover two, in the Mediterranean region.

In July 1961 I flew out to cover the small-scale war which had broken out on the Mediterranean shores of North Africa, between the Tunisians and the French. The two countries had held an uneasy peace since Tunisian independence in 1951 and the latest trouble had been sparked off by the Tunisian take-over of an old French naval base in the port of Bizerte.

Together with three other journalists I attempted to drive directly from Tunis to Bizerte, a journey of some 60 miles along the coastal road. The first part of the trip was easy, with very few reminders that we were in a war-torn country. But as we approached our destination we learned that Bizerte was surrounded by French paratroopers, and we saw several *Mystères* flying menacingly over the city. Suddenly, from a clear blue sky, one of these planes screamed its way towards us and we scrambled out of the car and dived into a ditch, landing among frightened farmers who were fleeing the fighting. I hollered out in agony as I fell onto a particularly prickly cactus. There were three or four similar incidents and eventually we gave up trying to reach Bizerte and drove back to Tunis.

Next day, I attempted the same journey again, this time in the company of a BBC correspondent and a fellow *Daily Herald* man, Dennis Eisenberg. Everything went well until we reached the river forming the No-man's-land between the opposing lines. The only way across was on board an old ferry boat tied up at a jetty and guarded by a patrol of French soldiers. The boat's crew were sheltering nervously inside and were, quite naturally, reluctant to take us to the other side. However, they had little choice but to obey the French sergeant in charge.

But it was a slow drag across that river, even with the engine at full power, and when we did eventually reach the other side we were caught for a few agonizing moments in the crossfire.

We moved quickly away from the danger, along deserted streets, leading towards the walled, inner city area where the Tunisian forces were dug in. Turning a corner we found ourselves face to face with a dozen or more Tunisian soldiers who raised their rifles to the 'aim' position the moment they saw us. I threw my hands into the air, thinking 'Christ! This is it!' and expecting the bullets to start ripping into my chest. The BBC man called out in French, 'Don't shoot – English journalists.' The soldiers lowered their guns and the moment passed.

We continued warily, dodging from door-way to doorway through streets where walls were riddled with bullet-holes and shop-fronts had been blasted out, with their window-glass lying smashed on the pave-ment.

I got separated from the others for a while. A friendly shopkeeper, obviously pleased to see a neutral person, beckoned me into his shop and offfered me some refreshment. I was feeling hot, and tired, and dirty and gladly accepted his offer. He took me into the shop where his small chil-dren – there were about four of them – were playing happily beneath a table. Like most of the kids I've seen in war-time, they seemed unaffected by all the turmoil raging around them. I took a drink from the man and laughed with the children for a few moments, then I went back into the street and rejoined my companions.

We met up with a young medical student who wore a Red Cross armband. He insisted on showing us the nearby hospital where he had been working and there we saw the

On the road to Bizerte a father and his two daughters flee from the fighting, 1961

grisly results of the fighting; the blood-stained uniforms of the overworked doctors and nurses; the injured and the dying.

We made the treacherous journey back to Tunis, and after sending our copy and films back to London we began to relax again. But next morning I awoke to find that my leg had turned septic. A cactus needle, from my fall in the ditch two days earlier, was still embedded in my calf. Being a bit of a do-it-yourself medic by this time, I bought a bottle of surgical spirit and lanced the infected area with a razor blade. The wound healed up within a day or two.

The French had gained control of Bizerte when I returned there. Spent bullet-cases littered the streets, and the French soldiers sat around outside the cafés drinking beer and wine, with bandoliers slung across their shoulders.

I came across the shopkeeper who had given me a drink a few days earlier. He was lying dead beneath a pile of rubble which had once been part of his shop. Outside on the pavement each of his children lay dead, too, their bodies covered by blankets with their heads and feet protruding from either end. They looked as though they were sleeping.

That night, back in Tunis, feeling totally disgusted by the whole dirty business of war, I drank too much and I cried a little. In the cold light of the new day I told myself that I'd have to be far less emotional if I was going to survive as a newspaperman.

Christmas-time 1963 saw renewed fighting in Cyprus between the Greek and Turkish factions who had been unable to settle their differences following Independence in 1959. My old friend Derek Lambert had joined the *Daily Express* by then, and we covered several stories on the island together. (By far the most horrifying of these occurred when the Red Cross asked us to witness the excavation of a field where they suspected several massacred Turkish villagers to be buried. After just a few shovelsful of earth, their worst suspicions were confirmed and the first of the decaying bodies was pulled

from the ground.)

Ever since my brief sojourn in Cyprus before the Suez crisis, I had held a special affection for the island, and during the course of my work I've since been there more than 20 times.

Whenever possible I stayed at the Ledra Palace Hotel – during the late fifties and early sixties, the number one meeting-place for journalists who were either covering the Cyprus troubles or simply 'Middle East watching'.

It was a comfortable refuge from the heat and a first-class watering hole, a superb Brandy Sour being the speciality of Sterio, the head barman. Then there was Savas, the hall porter – whom I'd met briefly in 1956 – nicknamed 'News Editor', because he seemed to know something about everything going on in Nicosia. Savas was a perfect Mr Fixit; whenever he pointed one in the direction of a good story, his information invariably proved to be correct. He later moved on to finer things in another hotel.

During the Cyprus troubles it was normal practice for us photographers to take our films to a small camera shop in nearby Ledra Street, for developing and printing. However, since Ledra Street had been nicknamed 'Murder Mile' by British soldiers following several shooting incidents there, this became a dangerous chore. In order to minimize the risks involved I decided to convert my bathroom at the hotel into a darkroom. The air-conditioning system would keep it cool and make it a reasonably comfortable place in which to work. At least that is what I thought.

My colleagues soon got to hear of my plan. They insisted on sharing the makeshift darkroom with me and on its very first day of operation six of us returned at midday, hot, tired and very thirsty, from a hard morning's work. Armed with bottles of cool beer we crowded into my room, pulled the curtains and got down to work.

Joe Joseph of the *Daily Mail* squeezed into the tiny bathroom with me to share the first turn. We didn't know it at the time, but the hotel's air-conditioning system, upon which rested the entire success of the oper-

Grivas returns in triumph to Athens, 1959

ation, was having little effect in the bathroom. Within minutes the temperature had risen to 90°F and the sweat was running off us in pints. Then we realized that the heat was having a disastrous effect on our films – the emulsion was beginning to melt! While cooling ourselves off under the cold tap we hit on the idea of obtaining a bucketful of ice in which to keep the next batch of developer cool.

Joe and I stepped out of the bathroom to find our four colleagues, similarly affected by the heat, stripped to the waist and about to remove their trousers. We stripped off, too, then I telephoned the bar to order two champagne buckets filled with ice. After a lengthy argument with the barman – who couldn't understand why I wanted champagne buckets without champagne – I eventually persuaded him to have them sent up.

A few minutes later a curious waiter arrived with the ice, and stared incredulously at the sight before him – six sweaty Englishmen in their underpants, socks and shoes, with the curtains drawn in broad daylight! He quickly handed me the buckets and left, probably wondering what we intended to do to one another with the ice cubes. After much swearing and a lot more sweating we did manage to develop all our film, but I always had the darkroom/bathroom to myself after that.

After the signing of Independence in February 1959, the exiled ex-EOKA leader Archbishop Makarios returned to Cyprus in triumph to take his place as head of the government. Thousands of his loyal supporters lined the streets of Nicosia to greet him, chanting 'EOKA! EOKA!' I took a picture of his marvellously photogenic, bearded face as he peered over the sand-coloured stone balcony of the Presidential Palace, waving to the crowd below.

Speculation quickly arose concerning the possible return of another EOKA hero, General George Grivas, for whom the British had been searching for the past two years. His Pimpernel-like disappearing act had become a source of great embarrassment to the army and they had finally put a huge reward on his head. It had never been claimed.

Now that the troubles were supposedly over, the *Daily Herald*, like several other newspapers was eager to capture Grivas's exclusive story of his hide-and-seek existence. I received instructions from London to join reporter Joe Vodicka in Athens where Grivas was expected to arrive at any moment. After several frustrating days, which I spent seeing the sights of the city, Grivas finally flew in, from Corfu, to be greeted with much pomp and ceremony by generals, admirals, politicians and a rather scruffy-looking guard-of-honour.

As Grivas stood at the top of the aircraft steps, dressed in a khaki beret, gaiters, brown boots and a baggy jumper secured around the middle by a Sam Browne belt, he reminded me of Charlie Chaplin in *The Great Dictator* and I found it difficult to believe that this little character had not so long ago caused so much trouble to the British Forces.

It was a great day for Grivas; he was the hero of the hour. But whatever hopes he held for leadership of the new Cyprus, he was destined to remain in the shadow of Makarios. Grivas eventually faded into obscurity and he died in 1974.

In June 1974 I was in Cyprus again for an exclusive photo session with Archbishop Makarios. By then the political situation had improved somewhat and Cyprus seemed to be enjoying peace and prosperity at last. Fine hotels had been built in places like Famagusta, Limassol and Kyrenia and many European holidaymakers were coming to enjoy the delights of the island. Now, tourists, instead of newspapermen, were to be seen drinking the Brandy Sours at the bar of the Ledra Palace.

Archbishop Makarios strolls in the gardens of the old Government House, Nicosia, 1974

Archbishop Makarios, as photogenic as ever, was dressed in his familiar flowing black robes though his black beard was now flecked with grey. I was surprised to find that, for all the power he wielded, he was a gentle man and was helpful and obliging as he posed for me beneath the arches in the beautiful gardens of the old Government House.

Two weeks later I was sitting in the Photographers International office, listening to the 9.00 a.m. BBC radio news, when it was announced that trouble had flared up once again in Cyprus. Archbishop Makarios was believed to have been assassinated, and Nicos Sampson – another ex-EOKA freedom fighter, once sentenced to death by the British – had taken control of Cyprus. There had been much fighting in the streets of Nicosia and there was a possibility that the Turks might take advantage of the situation and launch an invasion of the island. Together with my then partner, Paul Sergent, I quickly set to work and soon had several commissions to cover the situation for various newspapers.

By 11.30 that morning I was airborne, heading for Beirut – the best approach, as all civil air traffic into Cyprus had been banned. Within minutes of booking into the Palm Beach Hotel there, I was joined by many other journalists, all similarly faced with the problem of how to get into Cyprus.

A Cyprus Radio news bulletin announced that Archbishop Makarios had not been killed after all, thereby making for an even more interesting situation.

Next morning the airports of Cyprus were still closed. So, together with *Daily Mirror* foreign correspondent, Don Wise, and *Daily Express* photographer, Harry Dempster, I began to search for some alternative means of crossing that short stretch of the Mediterranean.

Don went off to the Harbour Club, hoping to persuade the owner of a luxury yacht to make the trip, while Harry and I went down to the dockyard. After many rude and aggressive refusals, we found an Egyptian skipper willing to make the crossing on his dilapidated cargo boat. However, he still had to unload his cargo of timber and would not be ready to set sail until the evening. He added that the fee would be £4,500. Whether he expected us to pay that much, I'll never know, for I simply said: 'Yes' and agreed to meet him in the afternoon to hand over the money. I had just £200 on me at the time!

Harry and I rang around all the hotels and bars in Beirut rounding up the journalists who wanted to make the trip, while at the same time telling them how much it would cost. Despite the fact that we'd heard that any seaborne attempt to enter Cyprus was likely to be fired at, we soon had enough passengers to pay for the hire of the boat.

Late in the afternoon we met the skipper and the owner of the vessel in a hot and sticky office on the quayside and one by one, the journalists paid their share of the fee. The skipper did a roaring trade and gave me what he thought was a generous discount of £20 on my own fare.

By embarkation-time I was feeling very wound-up and couldn't wait to get going. My frustration manifested itself when a taxi pulled up on the quayside, carrying several cans of unexposed ciné film which a French TV news-film crew had left behind in a local cafe. With a wave of his hands one of the Frenchmen, already on the boat, arrogantly ordered me to bring the film aboard. In my anger I picked up all the reels and flung them into the sea. Unfortunately one of the cans struck a Norwegian reporter on the head and knocked him cold. Luckily he recovered quickly, but was to nurse a sore head for the rest of the voyage. Needless to say pandemonium broke out and there was a near punch-up as some of the Frenchmen tried to recover their film.

We set sail just before dusk, colliding with another ship and destroying part of its bridge before leaving the harbour. To end a perfect day we slept out in the cold on the open deck.

Next morning we sailed, under the flag of Egypt, into the mouth of a silent Famagusta harbour; there was hardly a movement on the shore and we photographers peered through our telephoto lenses waiting for something to happen, while the reporters got in touch with the authorities via the ship's radio. They were told that someone would be contacting us soon.

Three hours later a small welcoming party came aboard to greet us on behalf of Nicos Sampson, the new President of Cyprus, with whom a press conference had been arranged for the following day in Nicosia. Until then we were put into a luxury hotel, under guard, as 'guests' of the government.

Harry Dempster and I, suffering more than most from the strains of the past few days, decided to make our own way to Nicosia ahead of everyone else to see if anything was happening there. Next day we met up with a young English couple who had been enjoying a holiday in Famagusta when the trouble broke out. Now they just wanted to get away. They had discreetly loaded all their luggage into a hired Mini Moke which they intended to drive to the capital in the hope of catching a plane to London. We safely escorted them to Nicosia airport, then booked ourselves in at the inimitable Ledra Palace Hotel.

We took a taxi to the area around the Presidential Palace, and it was immediately apparent that most of the fighting had happened there. The Palace itself was badly damaged (as was the old Government House where two weeks earlier I had met Makarios). We were about to start taking pictures when a lone soldier pointed an automatic rifle in our direction and ordered us away.

We were still pictureless and I remarked to Harry that we didn't seem to be getting much return for all the trouble we had taken so far.

Our colleagues soon arrived at the Ledra Palace and we joined them for the afternoon's press conference with Sampson, whom I had last met in the late 1950s when he had been working as a journalist for one of the island's newspapers. Now, surrounded by a battery of cameras and tape-recorders, he was the centre of attention as he showed off whips and other instruments of torture which Makarios's police force had

allegedly used on various prisoners opposed to their government. Although limited to the usual press conference shots showing the chief participant facing a line of microphones, I had something 'in the can' at last.

Next day, Friday, the press party was due to go on an officially conducted tour of the battle areas which Harry and I had already visited: a complete waste of time as far as I was concerned.

Instead of joining the tour I followed my intuition and, hiring a car, I drove north to Kyrenia, a picturesque fishing port facing the Turkish mainland. I intended to take a quick look around, then return to Nicosia that evening. But some second sense, a premonition perhaps, told me to remain overnight in Kyrenia where I booked in at the Dolphin Hotel.

That night I dreamed of flashing lights on the horizon. I awoke in a cold sweat at 4.30 a.m., I got up and crossed to the window. Sure enough, there on the horizon were several points of light blinking through the early morning mist. On top of the UN post situated in front of the hotel, a couple of soldiers were also peering at them through binoculars. After a while the mist began to clear and I was able to make out the shape of several ships in the distance. They were Turkish warships.

I went up to the hotel roof to look at the lights through my 300-mm telephoto lens. I saw several landing-barges bobbing up and down beside the warships. Then I heard the distant roar of a jet. I found the plane in my viewfinder and knew it was about to attack. It did, with rockets that blasted at the castle which overlooks the harbour. A second jet followed, with a rat-tat-tat of machine-gun fire, and then two bombs fell a couple of hundred yards from the hotel.

Then the jets turned and flew out to sea again. Their noise died away and I could hear quite plainly the crying of frightened people rudely awakened by a war.

I telephoned the Ledra Palace Hotel, hoping to contact Brian Parks, a *Daily Mail* reporter staying there. From the nonchalant way in which my call was answered, I knew that things were still quiet in Nicosia. I was put through to the wrong room, and woke up a tourist who was naturally very upset by my intrusion. 'Christ! He'll really have something to be annoyed about in an hour or so,' I thought. I got through to Brian after that and as I explained the situation to him Kyrenia came under attack again. Brian said he would grab a taxi and join me as soon as he could. I put down the phone, hoping that he would arrive before the Turks did.

I took another look from the rooftop and saw the barges approaching the shore farther along the coast, at a place called Five Mile Beach.

Back inside the hotel I advised the guests to stop using the lifts in case of electrical failure, and to fill all the baths with water in case the plumbing system got damaged by the firing. I also advised them to lie low or go to the cellar until the shooting died down.

A volunteer Greek militia man was resisting the pleas of his mother not to go to the war, while a young barman, to whom I had spoken the night before, was already dressed in a ridiculous ex-British Army surplus uniform and raring to go. Outside, the attacks continued with an alarming regularity.

Brian finally arrived and we decided to drive towards the scene of the landings. The young barman asked us to give him a lift up to the front line and the three of us set off towards Five Mile Beach, with Brian driving so that I'd be free to take pictures.

Every so often we had to slow up as Brian steered the car around debris left by the air attacks. As we approached the bay, Brian said, 'Just listen to those stones!'

'They're not stones,' I told him, 'they're bloody bullets! Someone is shooting at us!'

With that, Brian drove even faster towards Five Mile Beach, where we could see the Turkish barges nearing the beach. The young barman asked us to stop, then he jumped out of the car and ran off toward the hills, carrying an old .303 rifle in his hands.

We continued until we came to a block of flats overlooking the beach. Brian turned into the courtyard, where a sign read 'Kamares Palace Apartments'. We parked our car and entered the buildings where we found more than forty bewildered holiday-makers sheltering in some half-built garages, protected at the rear by a hill and at the front by the apartment building itself. We soon discovered that 24 of the occupants were British, the rest being German, Austrian or Dutch, and many of them still finding it difficult to believe what had happened. They were stuck in the middle of the fighting, with the Turks firing from the beach and the Greeks replying from somewhere behind the apartments. Another round of gunfire was enough to convince Brian and me that we, too, were pinned down and that it would be unwise for us to even attempt to drive around anymore.

After hanging out white sheets as flags, to signify our neutrality, we decided to make the garages as comfortable as possible by dragging in mattresses which we found in a store-room, and collecting water from the cistern in the basement. We then gathered together as much food as we could find, including loaves of stale bread, tins of frankfurters, cucumbers, fruit and anything else we could lay our hands on.

Suddenly, three dust-covered Greek soldiers burst in on us, carrying a seemingly injured comrade in their arms. We asked them not to involve us so that we could retain our neutrality. They said they'd go if we would take care of their injured companion, a scared teenager who was suffering from nothing worse than a bad attack of nerves. We agreed and relieved him of his rifle and his uniform, then left him to sleep it off in one of the garages.

We made our sleeping arrangements for the night: the women and children in the most protected area at the back of the garages and the men at the front. But, of course, it was impossible to sleep amid all the firing. Despite the fact that every so often we called out, 'Don't shoot – English' the noise continued spasmodically throughout the night.

As Sunday drifted in we could see the sky above the garages tinged red by the light of fires on the hillside above the Turkish bridgehead. A little later the bay was blanketed by a thick cloud of smoke. Later still a shell landed with a massive crash between the garages and the apartments, covering everything and everyone with dust but luckily no one was hurt.

In the afternoon Brian crawled through to the office attached to the apartments and managed to put through a telephone call to the UN post in Kyrenia. After quizzing him about the size of the Turkish build-up, the official at the other end took down details of the people trapped in the flats and promised to pass them on to the authorities.

The gunfire continued through that long, hot day, but somehow everyone trapped in the garages managed to stay in good spirits. Out on the terrace we saw an old lady in a deckchair, reading an Agatha Christie novel. Only after much persuading did she agree to join the rest of us in the garages. She was Helen Kazantzakis, widow of Nicos Kazantzakis, the author of *Zorba the Greek*. In the garages two girls, who were twins from Beckenham, in Kent, were trying to enjoy their sixteenth birthday party.

As evening approached, an elderly local rushed in to collect his son who had worked in the apartments. The visitor told us how bad things were outside and advised us to stay put. He took his son and the frightened teenage soldier who had arrived the night before.

Our only contact with the outside world was a transistor radio which we tuned alternately to the British Forces Broadcasting Service and Cyprus Radio. Unfortunately the news they put out was rather disconcerting; it seemed that there was no immediate hope of rescue for anyone trapped on the northern part of the island, where we were.

We risked a look over the balcony at the front of the apartments and, to our horror, saw a hotel on fire about five miles away. Someone said it was the biggest and newest hotel along that part of the coast, and was bound to have been full of guests.

As dusk fell the rockets and strafing from the air suddenly stopped, only to be replaced moments later by heavy ground-fire which sounded every bit as bad.

Next day the firing drew closer and became heavier as the opposing forces closed in on one another – with us still trapped between them. It was only a matter of time before we would be overrun by one side or the other.

We collected everyone together and told them to keep their heads down.

At the height of the action Brian Parks courageously ran forward, stripped to the waist and carrying a white flag made from a sheet.

'Come back, you bloody fool,' I called. 'You'll get yourself killed!' But Brian took no heed of my warning and kept on running, shouting something about women and children. He managed to attract the attention of a small group of Turkish soldiers who responded by opening fire on the flats. Brian sprinted back towards the safety of the garages.

A short while later the same soldiers charged into our shelter. Yelling 'All out! All out!' they tried to push us towards some steps, and into the Greek line of fire. Naturally we refused to go, so they forced us all at gun-point back into the garages.

The shooting stopped around mid-afternoon. Everyone began to relax and the main body of the soldiers went off somewhere, leaving us under the guard of two very nervous soldiers. Within ten minutes of their comrades' departure one of their rifles accidentally discharged, knocking a large hole in the ceiling. But gradually these two rather simple guards became less jumpy. They began to talk to some of the holiday-makers and proudly showed off snapshots of their families back in Turkey. They shared our food, smoked our last cigarettes and allowed us to listen to news bulletins on the radio. The reassuring strains of 'Lillibullero' were followed by the BBC World Service news announcement that the Royal Navy were planning to rescue all Britons trapped in Cyprus as soon as they could. We put out makeshift flags to ensure that the rescuers would spot our position. The twins and some other girls tore up sheets and with lipstick and eye-make-up turned them into

Union Jacks.

On Wednesday we witnessed the welcome sight of a Royal Navy helicopter coming in to land. A Chief Petty Officer explained to our guards that he had come to take us away. However, the two Turks refused to allow us to go, and the helicopter took off again leaving us feeling a little dejected while at the same time cheered by the knowledge that our release was being negotiated. A little later, a UN officer arrived in a jeep with a Turkish officer, then five more Royal Navy helicopters flew in for a mass landing. This time the Turks gave us up without argument.

'Bless them,' said one of the English women, 'they were only doing their duty!'

Brian and I were among the last to be lifted out. We spent the night on board HMS

Devonshire and were then transferred to the RAF base at Akrotiri. Within minutes of arriving there we were told that an RAF VC10 was about to take off for England. Four-and-a-half hours later we landed at Brize Norton in Oxfordshire.

I telephoned June in my usual cheerful manner: 'Hello, sweetheart. I'm sorry I haven't been in touch, but . . .'. I was about to tell her the incredible story of the Kamares Palace Apartments, but before I could continue, she burst into tears. Between the sobs she managed to say, 'You fool . . . we all thought you were dead. Don't you ever do this to me again.'

When I got home, it was difficult to tell which of us looked worst. I was still dressed in the same clothes in which I'd gone to Kyrenia six days earlier. I was dirty and

Making Union Jacks, Kamares Palace Apartments, 1974

Holidaymakers are evacuated by the Royal Navy

unshaven and feeling very tired. Poor June was a nervous wreck, totally drained of emotion. She told me that the *Daily Mail* had been in touch with my partner Paul Sergent to tell him that they had made unsuccessful enquiries at the Foreign Office and of the various UN units in Cyprus as to our whereabouts. No one knew we were alive, until we'd returned out of the blue.

Three weeks later I took an early morning walk in the Surrey hills which surround my home and the offices of Photographers International. I was searching for edible mushrooms and other likely fungi; it was one of the crazes to which I'm prone, every now and then. Not wanting to poison myself or my family, I'd even bought a book on the subject. However, it wasn't a toadstool which poisoned me that morning, but a small adder lurking in the undergrowth. At first the bite was no more than a mild irritation, but throughout the morning my hand began to ache.

Meanwhile news was coming in of renewed fighting in Cyprus. The Greeks and Turks were at it again, with the Turks gradually taking control of the northern sector of the island.

By lunch-time I was at Heathrow airport (en route to Sofia in Bulgaria where I planned to catch the famous Orient Express to Istanbul, then I was to drive to Ankara, and finally fly from there to Kyrenia on a Turkish military helicopter). I visited the airport medical unit and had a dressing put on my hand which had become extremely painful by then.

At Heathrow I joined up with a BBC-TV film crew who were also travelling the roundabout route to Cyprus. After we landed in Bulgaria the world-wide fame of the BBC was to become very useful as we waited for the Orient Express at Sofia's main railway station. We had arrived there in the warmth of a sultry evening, hungry and thirsty, only to find that the station restaurant was closed.

We piled our luggage on the platform and settled down for an hour's wait before the Orient Express arrived. Soon a curious crowd had gathered around the luggage and was muttering 'BBC . . . BBC . . .' with the result that the restaurant was re-opened for us and a very nice meal served up.

The Orient Express was far from the luxurious train I had expected it to be. It had little of the splendour and comfort that is seen on film. The restaurant car was a primitive affair, like a goods-wagon with old tables and chairs strewn around and an iron coal-stove on which the cooking was done.

We arrived in Istanbul some 18 hours after leaving Sofia, then hired a car to take us to Ankara, where we booked into an hotel.

By now my hand had swollen to the size of a grapefruit and was so painful that I could hardly touch it. There were no doctors available until the following day, so I took a new razor blade and, in my usual fashion, lanced the swelling. My blood spurted all over the bathroom, but the relief was

instant. One of the BBC men, who had gone off to find me some ointment, came in at that moment and turned a couple of shades whiter when he saw what I'd done.

We took off on board a Turkish army helicopter from the mainland, and finally landed in Kyrenia. I went back to the now-deserted Kamares Palace Apartments where the mattresses still lay in the garages alongside empty frankfurter tins and the broken eyebrow pencils which the girls had used to paint the Union Jacks.

I came across the young barman-soldier who I believe was the same man Brian and I had given a lift to three weeks earlier. He was dead, still wearing his British Army surplus helmet, and reduced almost to a skeleton. He wasn't far from the spot where we'd left him and must have been killed soon afterwards. I reported my find to the Turkish authorities, now firmly in command of

Kyrenia, with solitary Turkish guard, 1974

the north of the island, and they promised to recover the body and give him a proper burial.

That afternoon I went back to Kyrenia, which I'd always considered to be one of the loveliest places in the world. The port was virtually untouched by the fighting. The fishing boats still bobbed up and down at the quayside but the place was deserted, save for a solitary Turkish soldier, wearing a ridiculous helmet, marching up and down guarding the strange silence: it was an image which inexplicably turned me off Cyprus forever.

7

The Middle East Conflicts

1967 was a traumatic year for me, both personally and professionally. My personal life was in what can only be described as a bloody mess as I was involved in a disastrous emotional situation, all of my own making. It had begun two years earlier when I'd fallen in love with another woman, thereby placing my relationship with June under an intolerable strain. Inevitably there came a breaking point, when I left home and moved in with another photographer. I still had a great love for June and our girls, but there seemed nothing else I could do.

I mention this very personal problem only because it played an important part in my professional life that year. An overwhelming preoccupation with my emotions gave me, I believe, a couldn't-care-less kind of attitude towards death, consequently I took more risks in the pursuit of pictures than I might otherwise have done.

On a frosty February evening, June and the girls came to see me off from Gatwick airport – I was flying out to Aden to cover the troubles there. The farewell was a tearful occasion – although the tension was relieved a little when daughter Sally, then only seven years old, fell into the display of toys in the airport shop, sending them flying every-

where. June and I picked up the toys together and I promised that I'd return in a week or two, to sort out our problems once and for all.

I didn't come home again for seven months.

I landed at Aden's Khormaksar airport and was met by an Army Press liaison-officer who drove me to the Crescent Hotel at Steamer Point. On the way we passed through Maalla, a district where many British families lived in tall blocks of flats. Every now and then we passed small fires smouldering in the streets. The officer told me they were the remains of an Arab demonstration against the British, held the day before.

That short journey set the tone for the remainder of my stay in Aden.

My unfortunate bathroom/darkroom experiences in Cyprus had taught me a few lessons about hot countries, and since Aden is one of the hottest cities on earth – the intense Middle Eastern sun is reflected back on it by the surrounding rocky hills – I requested a room at the Crescent with proper air-conditioning. I was taken to a small room in the annexe where I immediately blocked out all daylight with black paper and tape, pulled the curtains and turned the air-conditioning unit to full power. During my stay at the hotel the room temperature remained at a constant 68°F and coming in from the outside was like walking into a fridge. I even slept with extra blankets on the bed, yet a walk along the corridor outside would make me perspire enough to soak my shirt to the skin.

For several days I was the only newspaperman in town and I spent my time getting the lie of the land. Then I was joined by Don Wise, of the *Daily Mirror*.

Don and I were dining together one evening when someone came in with the news of a bomb explosion in the Sheik Othman district at the home of Abdul MacKawee, a prominent Adenese minister. MacKawee's three sons had been killed in the explosion.

We drove out there, but could see nothing in the darkness. On the way back we discussed the implications of the bombing. Don summed them up (accurately, as it turned out) when he said: 'The shit will really hit the fan now!'

The funeral of MacKawee's sons was scheduled for the following afternoon in Crater, a highly populated area nestling in what remains of a long-extinct volcano. In the morning a general strike was called in the city as a protest against the killings. Two rival nationalist groups – the Front for the Liberation of South Yemen (FLOSY) and the National Liberation Front (NLF) – were blaming each other for the attack, and some rumours even implicated the SAS, who were known to be working in the mountains.

Despite the fact that we knew Crater to be a particularly dangerous place for Britons to enter, Don and I were determined to cover the funeral. Our plan was simply to wait in the street and watch the procession pass by. We drove around the outskirts of Crater, listening to the chanting of an angry crowd who were not far away, and as we parked our car beside an Indian trader's shop, several shots rang out in the distance. Half-jokingly we asked the shopkeeper to keep an eye on the car until we got back.

We stationed ourselves in one of the main streets near the cemetery and I climbed onto a wall for a better view. That's when I first saw the procession, hundreds of people heading towards us, but it was Don who first noticed that the leading group were dragging something along the ground. I looked through my telephoto lens and saw that it was the body of a man. They were tossing the torso carelessly into the air then kicking and beating it when it fell to the ground again. The poor sod must have been lynched but we were never able to find out who he was or why he had been killed.

Several youths suddenly broke from the crowd and ran towards us, shouting abuse, and what I now knew to be anti-British slogans. Don and I decided on the wisdom of the old axiom 'discretion is the better part of valour' and we made a hasty retreat.

By now we were cut off from our car by the crowd and decided that our best bet would be to head for the relative safety of the police barracks. However, an officer at the barracks – a rude and arrogant man – was preparing his men to go out to disperse the crowd and he more or less told us to 'get lost'.

Don had gathered enough material to write his story, and he decided to try to get back to our hotel. But I had taken hardly any pictures of note and decided to stay on. As Don walked away I heard some gunshots in the distance and began to run towards the sound, dodging every now and then for shelter behind the skinny trees lining the street. As I stood beneath one tree, a bullet whistled through the air clipping a few leaves off the branches above me.

Then I heard someone calling: 'Hold on, you silly bugger, I suppose I'd better come with you.' It was Don and I must say I was glad of his company.

We managed to get closer to the shooting, but there was nothing much to see. I resigned myself to the fact that I'd get no pictures that day and that it would be wiser to return to the Crescent, after all. Unfortunately we had unwittingly manoeuvred ourselves into an even more dangerous position and didn't know which way to turn for the best. But just then we saw a very welcome sight, red and white feathers in the berets of a patrol of Northumberland Fusiliers, who were moving in to secure the area. They'd arrived just in time like the cavalry in a cowboy film. They escorted us to the safety of their headquarters and then back to the spot near the cemetery where we had left our car. To our surprise it was still there and apparently untouched. The smiling shopkeeper saw us and came out of his shop.

'You know you left these in the ignition,' he said, waving the car keys at us. 'And the windows were wide open. This car might have been damaged with all these crowds about. So I locked it up for you, and kept an eye on it, just as you asked.' We thanked him and then, under escort, we drove out of Crater.

Soon afterwards a bomb exploded during a dinner party at the home of a British official. Two British women were killed, and several other guests injured.

By now *Daily Express* foreign correspondent Stephen Harper had arrived in Aden and gradually more and more journalists came in from all over the world as the situation worsened. Strange though it may sound, the troubles in Aden quickly settled down to a kind of deadly time-table around which we arranged our daily lives. Anti-British demonstrations were invariably held in the mornings before it got too hot; assassinations happened when people were travelling to or from work; bombings were the only flexible feature – they could happen anytime, anywhere.

At the Tarshyne Club where Stephen and I often breakfasted we sometimes received news of shootings or bombings, and off we'd rush to cover the incident. It was, I imagine,

Arrest in Crater's fish market, Aden, 1967

a bit like being in an RAF squadron during the Battle of Britain awaiting the order to scramble. One Sunday morning Steve and I joined a patrol of Northumberland Fusiliers in order to cover a demonstration in the market in Crater. We had been there just a few minutes, when someone yelled: 'Grenade!'

'Get that picture,' Stephen shouted as we dived for cover. 'You write the bloody stories and leave the pictures to me,' I replied as the grenade exploded nearby.

A couple of Fusiliers looked at us as though we were crazy. (That day Steve and I were to come under grenade attacks no less than three times.)

On another occasion in the same fish market, during yet another strike which had paralysed the city for two days, I was with two other photographers and the Northumberlands' chaplain, Jack Stacey. The stench of rotting fish, mixed with the acrid smell of water which had been poured onto burning blockades, was abominable. Only the flies seemed to be enjoying themselves.

I was talking to Jack when a sniper opened up with a burst of machine-gun fire. The bullets spattered into a wall behind us and the chaplain and I dived headlong into a pile of putrid fish-guts. A second burst followed, pinning us down so that we daren't move. 'At least I'm with the right bloke if

Trouble in Crater. An Arab lies dying and a British soldier injured following a grenade attack, Aden, 1967

I'm going to die,' I said. Jack's answer was lost in the noise of another burst of gunfire.

After a couple of minutes the shooting stopped and we scrambled clear, running towards the market building into which our companions had escaped. The two other photographers kept a reasonable distance from us as we all made our way back to the Fusiliers' headquarters, where, fully clothed, I stood beneath a shower scrubbing myself from head to toe with carbolic soap.

One night I was travelling with another journalist in a taxi, from the Yemen–South Yemen border back to Aden. We had spent the entire day following up the story of a prominent Adenese minister who was said to be hiding in Ta'izz (once, incidentally, the scene of the beheading of two SAS men, their heads having been exhibited on pikes in the main square). It was around midnight when we passed through rocky country in an area particularly notorious for its bandits. The 'road' was strewn with boulders, making it impossible to drive at more than 10 mph. Suddenly, against an *Arabian Nights* backdrop of bright stars on a black sky, we saw a single red light swinging to and fro across the road ahead. The taxi stopped and we waited in the stillness of the night. Then a gun-barrel was poked through the gap in the window beside my head.

'Fuck me!' was the only retort I could manage under the circumstances.

'Good job you said that, mate,' said the wielder of the weapon, in a voice as English as my own. 'Otherwise I might have shot you,' he added with a chuckle. His blackened face became visible in the gloom and I realized that he was an SAS man on patrol.

On the morning of 20 June, mutiny broke out among South Yemen forces working with the British in Aden. I was in Cyprus at the time, having just covered the Six Day War in Israel (more of that later) and was preparing to fly back to London that afternoon when I received a cable which read: RETURN TO ADEN TO COVER MAS-SACRE OF BRITISH SOLDIERS.

Khormaksar airport was closed to civilian traffic, but I managed to hitch a lift on an RAF flight via Bahrain and was back in Aden within 24 hours.

A series of macabre events had begun when men of the Royal Corps of Transport, returning to their headquarters on the morning of the 20th, believed they were in a protected area and unloaded the ammunition from their rifles as usual; but they came under heavy fire which left four of them dead, along with one unfortunate civilian who happened to be passing at the time.

The colony was put on 'Red Alert', which meant that the Northumberland Fusiliers, responsible for security in Crater, would take up a position in the armed police headquarters.

The mutiny coincided with the final days of the Northumberland Fusiliers' tour of duty in Aden. They were due to be replaced by the Argyll and Sutherland Highlanders, and that day were showing an advance party of Argylls around the district. As they turned into a side-road near the police barracks they, too, came under heavy fire from a Bren gun mounted on a rooftop. Only one man, a young Fusilier, survived to tell the tale of the massacre of his friends. Eight more soldiers, three of them Argylls, lay dead.

There were many grisly reports of the massacre. It was said that two injured soldiers were hanged in the main square while others were dragged through the streets and then mutilated. When the bodies were returned to the Argylls' battalion commander, Lieut-Colonel Colin Mitchell, they came in pieces in the boot of a taxi.

'When we go back into Crater,' Colonel Mitchell said to me soon afterwards, 'I'll take you with me.'

I covered the mass funeral of the Northumberland Fusiliers and the Argyll and Sutherland Highlanders (23 soldiers in all had been killed on 20 June). The setting for the funeral was the British Military Cemetery, surrounded by craggy hills, in a desolate place called Silent Valley. I watched the coffins being lowered into the graves and I saw the tears in the eyes of the young Fusiliers standing in the guard of honour. I was reminded of the Rupert Brooke poem which begins:

If I should die, think only this of me:
That there's some corner of a foreign field
That is forever England.

Even today I shudder whenever I think of that cemetery.

One evening a couple of weeks later I was leaving the Crescent Hotel with Stephen Harper and an AP photographer, Brian Calvert, when an Argylls' Land Rover pulled up alongside us and an officer called out: 'If you want a good story, follow me.'

'Christ! Everything happens at night,' I moaned as Brian and I hurried into the hotel to collect our cameras.

We followed the Land Rover to the back entrance to Crater, where Colonel Mitchell was briefing his men for an operation code-named 'Stirling Castle', after the Regimental Headquarters in Scotland. Beside him stood a pipe-major, complete with bagpipes.

'We'll be going in soon,' said the Colonel looking up at the darkening sky.

The Highlanders looked a formidable bunch; heavily armed, with bands of ammunition slung across their shoulders. Each wore his Glengarry at a jaunty angle on his head. But there was an air of trepidation about them for no one expected this to be an easy task. All the military experts had predicted that any British attempt to retake Crater would prove disastrous, with heavy losses.

When the night had properly settled on us we moved off in groups on both sides of the road, accompanied by armoured vehicles.

Funeral procession in Silent Valley following the massacre, Aden, 1967

The funeral of massacred soldiers, Silent Valley, 1967. The Northumberland Fusilier (foreground) holds back his tears

As we approached the bend before the courthouse, the humid night air was suddenly filled with the wail of Pipe-Major Robson's bagpipes skirling out the tune 'Campbeltown Loch'. The Colonel explained: 'We've been "entertaining" the locals with pipes and gunfire for several nights now. It's become a routine procedure. We'll surprise them with a bigger show tonight.'

'Campbeltown Loch' turned into 'Monymusk', the Regimental charge.

Moments later, all hell was let loose as both sides opened up. Tracer bullets scarred the night sky and machine-gun fire ricocheted off the rocks behind us. But the pipes kept playing: 'I wish that daft bastard would stop blowing the bloody things,' said a Scottish voice in the darkness.

Brian and I pushed forward from the shelter of an armoured car. In fact we went too far, and for a while we were lost. We saw some shadowy figures up ahead, but couldn't tell if they were 'Jocks' or Arabs.

I called out: 'Stirling Castle.'

Luckily they were Argylls. They led us back to the rest of the platoon.

The attack was all over very quickly. Operation 'Stirling Castle' was a success and we followed the Argylls to a building in the centre of Crater, which they made their headquarters for the night. Colonel Mitchell and his men had proved the experts wrong. Not one Highlander was injured in the retaking of Crater and only one Arab received a bullet wound.

I returned to the Crescent Hotel to develop my pictures and wire them back to the *Daily Express*. At dawn I went back into Crater to stand, uncomfortably, alongside the pipes and drums of the Regiment as they played rousing Scottish tunes on top of the tallest building in Crater. The Union Jack was raised in open invitation to any would-be snipers, but I believe the reputation of these tough men from the Highlands of Scotland had spread throughout Crater and no further trouble came that morning.

After breakfast Colonel Mitchell took Stephen and me on a tour of what were considered to be the most dangerous areas of Crater. To my surprise the local traders

Lt-Col Colin Mitchell (centre) with the Pipes and Drums of the Argyll and Sutherland Highlanders, back in the Scottish Highlands. Pipe-Major Robson stands in foreground

seemed genuinely pleased to see the Argylls. As the Colonel walked around in the market-places he was greeted at times by warm handshakes.

The retaking of Crater was a marvellous story for us. The British public love a hero and for his daring exploits Colonel Mitchell became known affectionately as 'Mad Mitch'.

Today Colin Mitchell is still a good friend of mine. He left the army soon after Aden, but later fought, successfully, to save the Argyll and Sutherland Highlanders from being disbanded. He became a journalist for a while and we later worked together in Vietnam.

In August I was thankfully relieved of the Aden assignment by another *Express* photographer, my old friend Stanley Megaher, who was sent out to cover the final withdrawal. After re-negotiations the British agreed to move out earlier than planned. The Union Jack was lowered for the last time in Aden, on 28 November 1967.

My stay in Aden had been interrupted in mid-May when I was sent to Cairo to produce some stories on Egyptian preparations for the possible forthcoming war with Israel. It was a frustrating assignment as the Egyptian authorities refused to give me adequate facilities for photography. This refusal stemmed, I believe, from President Nasser's displeasure at some journalists' reports and a certain cartoon which had appeared in the *Daily Express*.

However, I did manage to see something of these preparations when, for instance, Cairo was plunged into darkness one night as an air-raid practice took place. The only light came from the moon which bathèd the city in a romantic glow. Viewing the scene from the rooftop restaurant of the Cairo Hilton, I reflected that it was a sight many tourists would have willingly paid a small fortune to see.

I also managed to get permission to visit Port Said. It was a somewhat sentimental journey for me as I'd not been back there since the days of the Suez crisis. On the way I passed many broken-down Egyptian Army lorries and I remember thinking, 'If the rest of the army's like this, they stand little chance of winning a war!'

Port Said had changed a lot since 1956, but the Casino Palace Hotel was still there. I saw again the spot where I had almost tripped over the body of a British soldier and I walked around the billiard-room where I had witnessed the treatment of the wounded on those very tables, now faded with age. It all seemed so long ago.

On Friday 2 June, back in Cairo, I received a cable from the *Daily Express* foreign desk which read: JOIN RUTH IMMEDIATELY. I couldn't understand the message at first. Who the hell was Ruth? Eventually I figured it out. Ruth, an old Hebrew name, was Fleet Street code for Israel. I realized that they couldn't have said 'Go to Israel', as that would have placed me in an even more awkward position with the Egyptian authorities. I booked on the evening flight to Nicosia from where I intended to take the first available plane to Tel Aviv.

At Cairo airport I was given more than the usual 'going-over' by Customs and Security officials and my luggage was marked with a yellow cross, while that of other passengers went straight through. Consequently I arrived in Nicosia, while my luggage did not. I could go no further without it and there was little hope of it arriving until the next Cairo-to-Nicosia flight landed, on Sunday afternoon. I cabled the office to tell them of my predicament, then settled down to a free day in one of my favourite cities.

My luggage duly arrived on Sunday. The yellow chalk had been rubbed off, but each case had obviously been searched. My collection of cryptic messages written in Fleet Street cablese must have made interesting reading for someone and I tried to imagine what they would have made of things like: UP DATE ADEN PIX SOONEST . . . YOUR BYLINE SPLASHED PAGE ONE, or SENT FLOWERS TO WIFE OKAY. I felt like James Bond.

At 7 o'clock on Monday morning I presented my ticket at the check-in desk at Nicosia airport.

'I'm sorry, sir,' said the clerk, 'there are no flights to Tel Aviv.'

'Why not?' I asked.

A group of airport workers were crowded around a transistor radio nearby. One of them overheard my conversation and he pointed at the radio.

'You mean you do not know?' asked the clerk.

'Know what?'

'The Arabs and the Jews are fighting,' said the clerk. 'We do not know when we'll be flying there again.'

The airport worker looked at me. 'Yes. Very bad fighting,' he said, pointing at the radio again.

I sent a telex to the *Daily Express* asking what use I could be from Cyprus. The reply, from my editor at the Foreign Desk, was one of the most deflating messages I've ever received: OH DEAR YOU HAVE MISSED THE WAR RETURN LONDON SOONEST. It was worse than getting the sack. I tried to imagine the humiliation of going home with a reputation for missing a war. All my good work in Aden would be forgotten, for in Fleet Street you are only as good as your last assignment and in the eyes of my colleagues my 'last assignment' would be non-existent. I decided to ignore the cable and get myself into Israel, whatever the cost.

Luckily I wasn't alone. More and more correspondents had arrived in Nicosia, each with the same objective in mind. In desperation, some of us went to the Israeli Embassy to see if they could help. The

Overleaf
'The Victors and the Vanquished', Egypt, 1967

Ambassador promised to do what he could. On Tuesday afternoon he called to tell us of an El Al flight due to take off for Tel Aviv at midnight. We arranged for a ticket agent to come to the hotel where he sold us tickets at £25 each.

Just before take-off I telexed the *Daily Express* telling them I was on my way to join Ruth.

We were truly a jubilant bunch of newspapermen as our blacked-out plane came in to land at Lod airport, where Customs and Immigration formalities were kept to a minimum.

We quickly caught up with the story of the war so far. During the early hours of Monday morning the Israeli Air Force had simultaneously attacked every Egyptian, Syrian and Jordanian airfield, thereby rendering the air power of her enemies practically useless. It was a typical move by Moshe Dayan, and in less than three hours it had the effect of turning the tables in Israel's favour.

I was told that a Press party would be leaving, on a bus, at dawn, bound for the Sinai Desert. I decided to join the group.

The bus was crowded with many reporters and photographers whom I'd never seen before; one of the few I did know was UPI photographer Peter Skinley. We saw little evidence of the fighting until we passed through the Gaza Strip. After that the bus pulled up every so often beside burned-out Egyptian tanks and several of my travelling companions would leap out at each of these stops to photograph the scene. They reminded me of a bunch of tourists taking snapshots of some landmark; they seemed to be playing at being newspapermen. I really was glad of Peter's professional company.

It was a long and tiresome journey. We were already two days behind the war but eventually we arrived at El Arish where columns of smoke were rising from the town. In the town itself smiling Israeli soldiers, men and women, posed for our cameras, and waved their guns in the air while standing guard over captured Egyptian prisoners. At the El Arish airstrip I photographed Russian-built Egyptian fighter-planes lying wrecked beside the runway.

A short while later I took a photograph which, for me, sums up what that and all other wars are about. The picture shows an Israeli lorry crammed full with Egyptian prisoners-of-war, deprived of all dignity as they stand huddled together in their underwear. They are being taken away from the front line. Travelling in the opposite direction is a column of Israeli half-track vehicles, each filled with smiling troops on their way to the front. I later titled this photograph 'The Victors and the Vanquished'.

On the way back to Tel Aviv I learned of the death of Paul Schutzer, a *Life* magazine photographer with whom I'd been on several assignments in the past. He had been riding in an Israeli half-track when it was hit. The death of a friend in war makes you think about your own situation, your own vulnerability. Such news makes you tread more warily.

I was able to cover all fronts of the war during the next three days. I witnessed the tragic scenes at the destroyed Allenby Bridge, which crosses the river Jordan, as thousands of Palestinian refugees – old men, women, and children – attempted to carry their bundles of possessions across the broken structure to the relative safety of Jordan. (Since that day I've sympathized with the tragedy of Palestinian people caught up in what seems to me an insoluble problem. Today thousands of Palestinians still live in appalling conditions in refugee camps.)

In Jerusalem I saw the emotional scenes at the Wailing Wall, the only remaining part of a Jewish Temple destroyed 2000 years earlier by the Romans, as the first of the Jews arrived there to pray.

I received a cable from the *Daily Express* Editor, Derek Marks, congratulating me on my pictures from El Arish. They were to be spread over two pages in the paper. Naturally I felt pleased with myself and glad that my decision to ignore the cable recalling me to London had been justified.

Filled with new confidence I drove in a

hired Volkswagen, with a *Paris Match* photographer and my old mate Stanley Megaher, to the Golan Heights. Stanley, as he was in a natty pair of trousers, a sports shirt and a pair of fancy Italian shoes, was to my way of thinking ill-dressed for war. But he took my jokes, about being on holiday, in good part. As we approached the narrow road leading to the Heights we saw armoured vehicles pushing their way across fields, climbing like ants in zig-zag fashion between the white tapes marking a path through the concealed land-mines.

For us to get close enough to the action for photography meant driving along the same route between the tapes. But the tiny Volkswagen found great difficulty ploughing its way along the dusty track and I had to cross the tape several times to avoid getting struck or run over by a passing tank. Finally the car ground to a halt in the middle of a minefield. The advancing tanks literally had to squeeze past, until a soldier with a mine detector swept the area and moved the tape back a bit, enabling a freer flow of traffic. At the same time he marked two more mines about four yards away, over which we might have driven if the car hadn't stopped.

Stanley announced that he couldn't wait for a rescue vehicle and he set out on foot heading towards Quneitra and the front, while the *Paris Match* man went off in another direction. Although I wasn't too pleased at being left in a minefield I had no option but to stay with the car.

My throat was very dry, so I flagged down a passing half-track to scrounge some grapefruits from the crew. The Commander of the vehicle heard my English voice and told me that he came from Manchester. He offered to tow me out and within minutes the car was on the move again, even though the front bumper had been partly ripped off in the attempt.

I took some more shots of the Israeli advance, then drove on to a field-hospital where I learned of a new road back into Israel which had been recently cleared.

The *Paris Match* photographer rejoined me as daylight began to fade and we set out along the road behind a truck which was car-rying dead Israeli soldiers. After a mile or so we spotted a figure limping along the road ahead of us and I realized it was Megaher, looking like a bedraggled tourist. I drove straight past him and pulled up at a cafe some 200 yards farther on. I bought three cold beers and sat by the car with the Frenchman. Stanley arrived five minutes later, slumped down on a chair and took off his Italian shoes to reveal blistered and bleeding feet. He called me a few choice names for driving by when he was obviously in agony and I called him even choicer names for leaving me in the middle of a minefield. But of course he had been quite right to leave me for there was no point in two *Daily Express* photographers being stranded together; our first priority was the chance of good pictures and had our positions been reversed I would have done the same thing. We were soon laughing at the situation as we drove on down the road, with the bemused Frenchman wondering what we'd found so funny.

It took the Israelis just six days to re-draw the map of the Middle East and consequently the war became known as the Six Day War, a ridiculous title for a conflict which has, in effect, lasted for more than 2000 years.

I returned to England from Aden in August with my personal problem still unresolved. I was still in love with both women and wanted to hurt neither. The situation seemed likely to last for ever. In October I was sent to India to photograph the famous Maharishi Mahesh Yogi, who was wielding a great influence over the Beatles with his philosophy based on transcendental meditation. While staying at the Maharishi's home at Rishikesh near Delhi, I learned of fighting which had broken out in the tiny kingdom of Sikkim, on the Tibetan border, between Chinese and Indian forces. I heard that more than a thousand soldiers had been killed at the Natula Pass some 18,000 feet above sea-level. I returned to Delhi and applied to the Indian authorities for permission to go to Sikkim. This was granted a couple of days later.

As I was booking out of the hotel the concierge handed me two letters, both marked 'Express Airmail'. One was from June and the other from my girl-friend. I opened them and got the shock of my life, for both letters told me that the two had met at some hotel in London to discuss the situation. Both were asking me to sort myself out. Fast.

The problem occupied my mind for the rest of the three days' journey to Darjeeling, and up to the mountain capital of Gangtok from where I was driven by Land Rover up to the Natula Pass. As the Land Rover climbed up narrow roads overlooking rocky ravines, I kept wishing that it would topple over the edge and end my troubles once and for all. But it didn't.

We stopped at 18,000 feet up in the Himalayas, within sight of the Tibetan border. Beyond the barbed wire of the frontier a platoon of Chinese soldiers watched through binoculars as I walked towards them. The recorded voice of Chairman Mao echoed around the mountains to the tinny accompaniment of Chinese martial music, and his portrait gazed implacably into India. An officer perched high on a rock yelped out an order and further down the line a soldier took careful aim at me with what looked like an ancient Rolleiflex. Our shutters clicked at the same moment. I took a few more pictures before returning to the waiting Land Rover and leaving the Chinese to puzzle over who I was.

Back in London I booked into an hotel, feeling decidedly unwell. The strains and tensions of the past months had at last caught up with me. The *Daily Express* Picture Editor, Frank Spooner, told me I'd be better off at home and he sent a car to take me there.

June took charge and began to nurse me back to health. There were crisp white sheets on the bed, and delicious bacon and eggs to eat. The girls were pleased to see me and I was equally pleased to see them, to see how they'd grown. It was good to be home again, and I decided to stay.

*

On the morning of Sunday 7 October 1973 I joined a friend for a pre-lunch drink in a local pub. The landlord was surprised to see me.

'I thought you'd be on your way to Israel, by now,' he said.

The previous day Egypt and Syria had attacked Israel across the Suez Canal, recapturing territory lost during the Six Day War of 1967. The attack had come during Yom Kippur, a Jewish religious holiday, and had taken the Israelis completely by surprise. I'd been thinking about the situation for some time earlier and had been unable to decide whether to go or not.

The landlord's remark seemed to unlock something in my mind, and I began to think that I'd perhaps misjudged the importance of the event.

Throughout lunch I sat glued to the radio, listening to the latest bulletins. I asked June to call Heathrow to check on the availability of flights to Tel Aviv. All flights had been cancelled except for one, which was due to take off in an hour-and-a-half's time and which was almost fully booked.

'I'm going to try for it, too,' I said, deciding suddenly that I should be in Israel.

I drove to the airport where a tremendous crowd were arguing excitedly with the El Al ticket-staff. I saw many of my Fleet Street colleagues pushing and shoving, along with hundreds of Israelis anxious to get home. It was impossible to get anywhere near the ticket-desk so I slipped away from the crowd. I bumped into an airline official whom I'd met several times in the past. 'Aren't you Terry Fincher of the *Daily Express*?' he asked.

I told him I was Terry Fincher, but left out the fact that I had left the *Express* and was now freelancing. I explained my difficulties about getting on the flight and he said he could help me. He whisked me through Customs to the departure lounge where he told me to wait while he went off with my credit card to get my ticket. Within forty minutes of arriving at Heathrow, I was seated on board the plane and on my way to cover yet another Middle Eastern war. I could hardly believe my luck!

Many of my friends had managed to get on

board, too, including Brian Parks and Monty Fresco, of the *Daily Mail*, and we agreed there and then that I should cover the war on a retainer for their paper.

The flight passed quickly as we swopped Fleet Street gossip over a few drinks and our landing at Lod airport was reminiscent of my arrival in 1967, with everything on the ground blacked-out.

We booked in at the Dan Hotel and decided to drive to the Golan Heights next morning where fierce fighting between the Syrians and the Israelis had been reported.

The surprise attack during Yom Kippur had left the Israelis with many casualties and there was now a marked difference in their attitude, to that which I had noted in the triumphant days of the Six Day War. I was surprised to see a great improvement in the road. The white tape tracks between the mines had been replaced by wide, open, tarmac highways.

Knowing the area reasonably well was a great help and we were among the few journalists who managed to get near the front that day. But it was tense up there. We were on our own in a bright red car, not knowing how far to push forward. We soon came to a stretch of reasonably straight, narrow road with expanses of Golan landscape on either side. We stopped the car and turned off the engine. Apart from the distant booms of artillery and the occasional screams of Syrian jets, there was an uncanny silence about the road, broken only by the odd whistle of birds in the long grass. There is a sixth sense, honed to perfection by long experience of war, that I've felt about deserted roads in a battle-zone. Several of my friends have been killed travelling along such roads.

'There's no way I'm going down there,' I said. Brian and Monty respected my judgement and we turned back, never knowing if my decision had been right or wrong.

I decided to spend the second night on the Heights, while Brian and Monty drove back to Tiberias. I managed to get a lift with another photographer and we drove around, searching for a safe place to spend the night. It was a great relief when we found a forward Israeli armoured unit, for it was sui-

cidal to move around the Heights at night. The Israelis told us they were dug in for the night and made us welcome. One of them was an Englishman who gave me a cup of tea and some dry biscuits. As we sat beside his half-track vehicle he told me that their Intelligence reports suggested that the Syrians would attempt a big commando raid that night. Almost as he spoke the first incoming shell landed nearby with a deafening crash and we scrambled underneath the vehicle for shelter. Half an hour later the unit prepared to move out as the Syrians had pin-pointed our position. Their sergeant told me that we couldn't go with them so, in the dead of the night, the other photographer and I drove without lights to a safer position farther behind the lines, where we slept in the car.

We awoke next morning before the sun came up, feeling cold and damp. We drove back to the front where I photographed Israeli tank crews nervously saying their prayers before going into battle.

There was much more action that day, with fighter planes flying very low over the hills to avoid the deadly missiles which were taking a big toll of the air-power on both sides.

I had stopped to rest by a crossroads, when an Israeli tank, charging back from the front, pulled up beside a nearby medical unit. The crewmen gently lifted their Commander down from the tank. He had been hit in the throat by some rocket fragments. A shock of red hair sprang from his helmet as they took it off. I watched as the medics tried desperately to save his life, but he died within minutes. (Some months later I received a letter from an Israeli girl who had seen this photograph. She believed the Tank Commander to be her boy-friend. She told me that they had spent many happy hours together on the Heights; now she wanted to know the circumstances of his death there. I wrote back expressing my sympathy and telling her what I knew of the incident.)

A little later I photographed some Syrian tank-crew members lying dead beside their burnt-out tank, looking as though they were taking a nap in the sun.

The Israeli authorities were insisting on developing all film and censoring any pictures showing their countrymen lying dead, which I thought was a ridiculous order. It is impossible to report a war without showing the truth and from *both* sides. I knew I had to try to get my material away uncensored.

I telephoned the airline and was told of a flight leaving for Rome later that evening. With a bit of swift manoeuvring I managed to get to the airport in time for take-off, leaving my exposed films lying among the rubbish at the bottom of my camera bag. I proceeded to sweat all the way through the Customs and Security checks. They were searching everything, even opening up the backs of cameras in a search for concealed weapons. Luckily they didn't sift through my paraphernalia and I was soon seated on board the plane with my films intact. Once airborne I ordered a couple of bottles of champagne and tried to relax. Since then I've had time to realize how lucky I was not to get caught 'smuggling' my films out. It is certainly something I'd never risk today.

I slept on the floor at Rome airport, then caught the first flight to London next morning. I took the films back to my darkroom and developed all the pictures. They were good and made much space in newspapers and magazines everywhere. The *Daily Mail* spread my pictures alongside Monty's in their centre-spread.

I stayed at home just long enough to have a bath and shave and collect some clean clothing, then I was on my way back to Israel.

Tel Aviv was now jam-packed with correspondents from all over the world. The big story was now centred on Sinai, where the Israelis had regained lost ground in a massive tank-battle.

The US correspondents were getting preferential treatment from the authorities, since their coverage would show the American people what was going on, and the Israelis desperately needed their support.

Unfortunately for me the papers from Europe, containing my pictures from the Golan Heights, had begun to arrive in Israel. The censor was not pleased and I spent hours trying to persuade the powers-that-be to give me a pass for Sinai. After much persuasion I eventually found myself in the company of two photographers and with permission to go to an advance Israeli camp somewhere in Sinai. We drove there through the night, finally arriving in the early hours of the morning at a camp shrouded in a damp mist, where we found the Press liaison officer fast asleep in a small office littered with plastic cups. As his sleepy eyes appeared from beneath the blanket his face seemed familiar to me, but I couldn't remember his name. He told us to get some sleep as we would be moving to the front line at first light. Remembering all the obstacles I'd encountered getting to Sinai it was a relief at last to hear something positive.

At dawn the Press liaison officer squeezed into our car and said he was to take us across the Suez Canal. He had a deep voice and a pleasant smile and, my curiosity overcoming my ignorance, I asked his name. He said he was Topol, the actor.

On the road to the canal we saw the results of the previous day's fighting and as we approached we heard the now familiar sounds of war. There was a rickety pontoon bridge across the canal which felt decidedly unsafe as we walked across it. On the Egyptian side, knocked-out Israeli tanks had been pushed aside to make way for the advancing army and the usual white tape marked a path through the mines.

We were joined by 20 or more other correspondents and Topol excelled himself by requisitioning a large, open-topped lorry from somewhere for us to travel around in.

We could see the war raging on either side of us as we drove towards the front line, leaning casually over the side to take our photographs. At times advancing Israeli tanks were driving alongside us, and every now and then we saw the snaking trails of Egyptian surface-to-air missiles as they tracked the elusive Israeli jets.

After a while Topol, in his role as chaperone, decided that we were too close to the fighting. He jumped down from the lorry and stood in the sand, like a traffic cop,

Dying Israeli tank-commander is lifted from his tank on the Golan Heights, 1973

directing us back to safety.

In the town of Suez we saw many Egyptian prisoners-of-war. Unlike their predecessors in the Six Day War, they knew the present Egyptian army had proved itself a force to be reckoned with and, even though captured, they gazed back at us with a look of pride and defiance.

We came to the pontoon bridge again just as a fresh bout of artillery shelling began. Topol took us to the safety of some empty trenches where we were stuck for almost an hour. The smell of burning filled the air about us. Topol went off somewhere to return a few minutes later with a crateful of soft drinks. He was the perfect host under the circumstances, and was very concerned for our safety and comfort: I didn't have the heart to tell him that I'd been under fire a few times before and was well used to such discomfort.

When the firing had stopped and darkness had begun to fall, my companions and I decided to risk crossing the pontoon bridge, back to our car.

In the dusk the white tapes were illuminated by small fires which seemed to be flickering everywhere. We reached the bridge safely, and wasted no time in crossing it.

The car was still there. I climbed into the back seat, closed the door and began to unload my cameras. That's when the next round of firing began. Hundreds of guns opened up at once and it looked like a spectacular fireworks display. I saw my fellow-travellers dive for safety underneath the car. I was desperate to join them, but couldn't open the door, which was fitted with child-safety locks. I wound down the window and squeezed myself through as fast as I could, landing flat on my face in the sand.

The shooting soon stopped and we were joined by others in the Press party, staggering back from the canal where they had been caught out in the open, not knowing whether to run or jump into the canal.

Back in Tel Aviv I took my films to the censor for clearance, then caught an afternoon flight back to London. I arrived back in England utterly exhausted, as I hadn't slept properly in ten days.

A cease-fire was called on 27 October which meant that I didn't have to go back to Israel. The Israelis had broken the back of the Arab assault begun on Yom Kippur.

The following Sunday I was walking once again in the Surrey countryside and I called in at the pub. The landlord had forgotten all about the problems in the Middle East.

'Hello, Terry,' he said. 'What have you been doing lately?'

'Oh, nothing much . . .' I replied.

8

Biafra

One lunch-time in 1968 I was sitting at the bar of the Blue Boar Hotel, in Cambridge, thinking that life had been a bit dull lately. I had returned a few weeks earlier from covering the Tet offensive in Vietnam (more of that later), and my current assignment was trying to photograph a female rabbit at the local agricultural institute. (Fertilized ova from a sheep had been transplanted into the womb of the rabbit and she was soon to be flown to Tokyo where the ova would be transferred to a Japanese ewe!) I had spent the entire morning attempting to get permission to carry out the assignment, but had met with little luck. As I sat there wondering whether to try again after lunch, the phone rang behind the bar. The call was for me. *Daily Express* Picture Editor, Frank Spooner, was at the other end with a note of urgency in his voice.

'Thought I'd find you there, Terry,' he said. 'Have you got your pictures yet? If not, forget it. You and René are booked on tonight's flight to Lagos.'

'It's on, then,' I said, referring to another item that had been in my thoughts. René McColl and I had recently been to the Nigerian High Commission in London for a briefing on the stance of the Federal side of

the Biafran war. The *Daily Express* Foreign Desk had taken their time in deciding whether or not to cover the conflict, and by now I'd expected to hear no more about the story.

'Yes, it's on,' said Frank. 'So forget the bloody rabbit and get back to the office as quick as you can.'

I rushed back to London, and the rabbit was presumably whisked off to Japan. I collected traveller's cheques and film-stock from the office, then jumped into a taxi for the airport where June met me with a hastily packed suitcase. I kissed her good-bye and then boarded the plane with René. He explained that our hurried departure was due to the fact that Port Harcourt had supposedly been retaken by the Federal Army and it looked as if this could lead to the final collapse of the Biafran forces.

The *Express* wanted us to move quickly. Knowing that part of the world fairly well, I told René that we'd be lucky to do anything quickly out there. In fact, after landing in Lagos it took three days before we could continue the next part of our journey from Lagos to Calabar on board a plane with several other journalists. Our progress was halted yet again in Calabar by the all-too familiar disputes between pressmen and over-officious Nigerians. Then, to make things worse, a bad storm blew up, delaying our departure on an old river-boat. We finally boarded the vessel and after two hours we were transferred to a Nigerian Army lorry and in the dead of night were taken along notoriously rough roads through war-ravaged country. Many bridges had been destroyed, forcing our driver to search for alternative routes. Every so often a Federal patrol would leap out of the bushes, and stand in front of our headlight beams, screaming: 'Stop!' while pointing their rifles straight at us. They would allow us to pass only when they were satisfied that we were on 'their' side.

Before reaching our destination we were forced to spend the night in a small village where we slept in a building once occupied by natives. It was infested with bugs and mosquitoes. One unfortunate reporter suffered acute discomfort when a worm ate its way into his leg during the night and the creature had to be removed by surgery when the reporter returned to Lagos.

We finally reached the Nigerian Army's advance tactical headquarters, which were under the command of Colonel Benjamin Adekunle, known in the press as the 'Black Scorpion'. He and his troops (the Marine Commandos, a so-called 'elite' corps, whose status in the war had grown to almost legendary proportions following several victorious sorties under their leader) had taken over a deserted mission previously occupied by an order of Catholic nuns.

Despite his small stature, Adekunle was an incredibly imposing figure. He wore a peaked hat covered in so much gold braid that it reminded me of dollops of scrambled egg. His uniform was immaculately pressed and his boots were shiny black. Above all he was photogenic, and a born actor, using a swagger-stick to punctuate his sentences as he spoke by smashing it against the side of his leg at appropriate moments. Every now and then he yelled at the tall sergeant-major who acted as his general dog's-body and who seemed to follow Adekunle everywhere like a shadow. The sergeant-major was over

six feet tall and he was dressed in an ill-fitting uniform, the trousers of which looked as though they'd had a serious argument with his boots, as their cuffs swung at least six inches above his ankles.

Whenever things went wrong in the running of the headquarters, Adekunle would bear down on his sergeant-major who, in turn, would swing around and bawl out whichever lower-ranked soldier happened to be standing nearby. It was clear that these Nigerian soldiers were highly volatile people and we realized that we had to tread lightly.

That afternoon my companions, including René, decided to return to Lagos as there seemed little likelihood of anything exciting happening around the headquarters. Trusting in my instinct I decided to stay on a bit longer. I had a feeling that I just had to wait and something would happen. None the less I felt a definite twinge of envy as I watched my friends depart.

When they had gone, I received a warning from Adekunle himself: 'You are now the only white man for miles – except for mercenaries,' he said. 'Step out of line, and I can have you shot.' He was grinning as he spoke, but, joke or not, I made a mental note to toe the line. I was placed in the charge of an officer, who turned out to be a kind and pleasant man.

That evening I was invited to dine with the Colonel in his quarters. Throughout the meal we drank a dull fermented concoction called palm wine which had the pallor and, what I imagine to be, the taste of sweet dish-water. Each time I finished a glassful Adekunle would offer a top-up. I thought a refusal would offend and so, dutifully, accepted each glass.

Background music was provided by Frank Sinatra and Glenn Miller records. They were obviously the Colonel's favourite entertainers. The moment one record finished Adekunle would flip it over again or change it for another. He was fascinated by stories of other soldiers and listened intently as I recounted tales of 'Mad Mitch' and the retaking of Crater in Aden. He wanted to know all about Vietnam and told me proudly that he had received his military training in

Moscow. Between courses he casually mentioned that he'd recently had to chastise some of his men for eating a Biafran. Whether this was true or not, I never knew, but my appetite certainly waned a bit at that point and I was glad when, at around 9 o'clock, Adekunle ordered me to take to my bed, as he had things to do.

I slept in a small room which had previously been occupied by one of the nuns. A cross hung crookedly on the wall. The chest of drawers had been emptied out onto the floor and discarded Bibles and prayer books lay in a heap in a corner. The palm wine had made me drowsy and I lay on the bed beneath a mosquito-net full of holes. Staring up at the ceiling I wondered if I'd made a mistake in staying on.

Early next morning I was eating breakfast with the officer on his veranda overlooking the courtyard, when a car and a Land Rover roared in and screeched to a halt outside Adekunle's office. The car doors swung open and two white men were dragged out and slung to the ground. I could see they were in a bad way as both their faces were cut and bruised and their clothes were torn. They had obviously been beaten. Two African prisoners were also thrown from the Land Rover. One had a broken arm which hung limply at his side and the slightest movement caused him to scream out in agony.

Adekunle stepped out of his office, followed closely by his sergeant-major, and marched up to the prisoners. The Colonel stood in front of the two white men, prodding them with his stick while issuing orders to his soldiers: I believe he thought the two men were mercenaries. The men, however, were in no position to protest and they took his anger in silence.

The officer with me could see that I was upset by what was happening, but advised me to sit still, warning that it would prove dangerous for me to get involved.

Down in the courtyard Adekunle and the sergeant-major walked back to his quarters. The prisoners were taken, across a sports field, to a place behind some wooden huts about a hundred yards away. It suddenly occurred to me that they might be walking to their execution and I knew I had to help them if I could. Then the officer was called to Adekunle's office.

When he'd gone I slipped a Leica beneath my shirt and made my way towards the huts near where the white men had been taken. None of the soldiers around the mission questioned my movements, as they had seen me about the place, unaccompanied, the day before. Behind the huts several soldiers stood guard over the prisoners. I moved forward, with my camera at waist-level, clicking off a few pictures as I walked – I dared not raise it to my eye.

'Can you speak English?' I asked the nearest white prisoner, thinking they might perhaps be German or Swedish.

'We are English,' he replied hoarsely as I slipped the camera beneath my shirt again. 'My name's John Downing and that's Bill Blakely.' He nodded in the direction of his unfortunate companion.

With that I heard the voice of the officer close behind me: 'You fool! I told you not to get involved. You are in trouble now. The Colonel wishes to see you, immediately. You'd better come now, at the double.'

I turned, to see Adekunle striding towards us across the field, the swagger-stick going twenty-to-the-dozen against his leg.

'At the double,' repeated the officer.

'I can't move any faster,' I said, 'I've hurt my leg.' This was partly true and partly a means of gaining time to think.

Adekunle was almost upon me. I knew I had to think quickly or the swagger-stick could be going twenty-to-the-dozen against the side of my head.

'What a good story,' I said, '. . . the way you have saved the lives of these men . . .' I gestured towards Downing and Blakely.

An agonizing moment followed as Adekunle turned the phrase over in his mind. He gripped the stick tighter and I braced myself, expecting him to bring it down on me. But, instead, he strode over to the prisoners and looked into their faces. 'Who has done this to you?' he asked.

I stood behind him signalling to the prisoners and mouthing the words 'Guards'.

British prisoners, John Downing (left) and William Blakely. The African prisoner (far right) has a broken arm. Nigeria, 1968

Luckily Downing caught my meaning: 'The guards . . . the guards did it,' he said.

Adekunle spun around and punched one of the guards who had brought the prisoners in. The guard fell to the ground and Adekunle began kicking him and jumping up and down on him. I whipped out my Leica and took more pictures. After a minute or so the exercise seemed to calm Adekunle and he ordered that the prisoners be confined for further questioning, then he fixed me with his steely gaze.

'To us,' he said, 'the only white men are mercenaries, serving the enemy. Therefore these men will have to be fully investigated.'

I turned my back on the prisoners while they were taken away.

Adekunle continued: 'Come, I will take you to Port Harcourt airport, now. And I will prove to you that I've taken it and won the war.' We walked on across the sports field.

I collected my other cameras from my room. Then, Adekunle and I climbed into the back of his staff car, a large white Peugeot. The tall sergeant-major jumped in beside the driver and the car lurched out of

the headquarters towards the airport.

In the boot of the car were a couple of crates of beer and champagne and each time Adekunle felt a thirst coming on he would order the driver to stop. The sergeant-major would then leap out, open the boot and fill his Commander's glass.

When we eventually reached the perimeter of the strangely silent airport my host stepped out of his car and said, 'I will show you my artillery positions.'

I crept quietly up a grassy bank behind the Colonel and the sergeant-major. On the other side lay several members of the elite corps of Marine Commandos, Gunnery Division, fast asleep beside a howitzer.

The Black Scorpion roared like a lion. He leapt over the bank and raced to the gun while the sergeant-major grabbed a lump of wood and began belting a surprised gunner with it. Adekunle tugged at the firing-string of the howitzer, but it came off in his hand. Then he struck the gun with his swagger-stick. Nothing happened. The sleepy battalion were quickly roused, however, and the firing began.

We drove on, past a few bodies which lay

4   DAILY EXPRESS, TUESDAY, MAY 21, 1968

White men bound, beaten up . . .

The Fincher File

TWO BRITONS, their faces welted from whip lashes, their wrists tied tightly behind their backs, were pulled out of a car at the Nigerian Federal Army's advanced tactical headquarters outside Port Harcourt. Mr. John Downing, 45, of Great Ham, Sussex, and Mr. William Blakely, 50, of Falcon Road, Edinburgh, had been captured outside the town.

Commanding the headquarters was strong-man Colonel Benjamin Adekunle. He took one look at the way the prisoners had been treated . . . then, furious, he grabbed the guard responsible. He ripped off the man's shirt, hit him, knocked him to the ground, and jumped on him.

Pictures by TERRY FINCHER

(Photographer of the year)

Story by RENÉ MacCOLL

Arms freed, but still under guard: Mr. John Downing and Mr. William Blakely await questioning before being sent on to Lagos

LAGOS, MONDAY.
HE CLAIMS to be the only true Nigerian. For in this divided, country he can boast a Yoruba father, a mother from the

What's more he can speak all four of the country's main languages.

Colonel Benjamin Adekunle, 30 years old last month, is a fantastic man. Flamboyant, full of panache, a born actor. With his hat covered in

just before the fall of vital Port Harcourt the other day, he was annoyed because one of the gunners manning a battery of howitzers had fired a few moments late, Adekunle nipped over to the luckless chap and gave him three of the best as a

palm wine, a dull grey fermented concoction which I do not recommend. Nostalgic Glen Miller melodies seeped from the Japanese stereo set in the corner.

Bed at 9 p.m.—and up the next morning at 4.30. Into

DAILY EXPRESS, TUESDAY, MAY 21, 1968   5

and the C.O. who hit out in anger

MR. JOHN DOWNING, who represents a tractor company, was on his way to fetch some fuel for his fridge when he was captured. Mr. Blakely, a marine manager, was sitting at home . . . waiting for the Federal troops to arrive. Both men were very distressed after their beating and suffered from shock.

For Mr. Blakely it has been a sad year. His wife whom he sent home to Britain for safety died soon after arrival.

In New Hampshire, America, his sister-in-law said: "This is tremendous news that Bill is safe. Mail has been sent to him in Biafra, but no replies have been received. We hadn't heard from him since last October."

Mr. Blakely's parents—in their eighties —are at present on a golden wedding trip to America.

Summary justice . . . the Adekunle way

The story as published in the *Daily Express*, 21 May 1968

by the roadside. Vultures perched on some of the carcasses pecking and pulling at the flesh.

We turned into the airport, which had been one of the last Biafran strongholds. I walked behind Adekunle along the runway and every few steps he would indicate a buried mine. 'Now you can report that the Nigerian Federal Army has retaken the airport,' he said proudly.

We returned to the mission where I noticed some vultures circling overhead, and then I saw a couple of dead bodies lying near a woman who was sitting against a wall. Around her sat three tiny children. The poor woman's meagre clothing was a mass of tattered rags and blood; her dress was torn and I saw three gaping bullet holes in her back. I drew Adekunle's attention to the wretched woman and a medical officer was sent to attend to her. But there was very little they could do for her with their inadequate medical facilities.

Some time later a helicopter landed. I believe it was the only one operating in the war and it was piloted by a Frenchman but commanded by a Nigerian Air Force officer, an arrogant bastard who told me he would not allow me on board. Adekunle overheard this and he looked the Commander straight in the eyes.

'I'm Colonel Benjamin Adekunle. I am in charge here. You will take my friend back to Calabar, and you will be nice to him – understand?' The Commander understood and I climbed aboard the helicopter.

As the helicopter rose I watched the receding figure of Adekunle beneath me. He gave one wave of his swagger-stick, then marched back towards the command-post.

I arrived in Calabar two hours ahead of René and the others, who had left me at the mission for the past 24 hours. They had been making the long trek by road. I told René the story of what had happened to me, stressing that we must contact the British High Commission immediately we got back to Lagos to ensure the safety of Downing and Blakely, but at the same time, we made the decision to tell the story to no one else.

On arrival back in the capital we went straight to the British High Commission. A deputy was on duty there and he promised to contact the necessary military authorities in Lagos, to make sure they were aware of the whereabouts of the two Englishmen.

A couple of hours later, after we had washed and shaved, René and I were relaxing with our companions when the deputy entered the room and proudly proclaimed to everyone that he had taken care of everything and, in the process, giving the complete story to our rivals.

René, who stood more than six feet tall, rose like some large giant from the table and bellowed: 'Fool!' at the unlucky man. Then, after René stormed off, there was a total silence. I explained the situation to our colleagues. Being professionals they understood our predicament and agreed to hold the story until after the *Daily Express*'s first edition, next day. Of course they didn't have any photographs, but I filled them in on all the details, so that when they got the call-back from their respective offices – which was to be in the middle of the night – they'd be equipped with all the answers.

In this way the story was still a big scoop for the *Daily Express*, and was spread over two pages.

A couple of days later John Downing and Bill Blakely were released into the care of the British High Commission.

I returned to London feeling unwell. My story had become big news back home, and June met me at the airport accompanied by a BBC-TV car to take me to the studios where I was to appear on a late-night news programme to talk about the incident. After the interview I collapsed, suffering from a bout of malaria.

I went back to work some weeks later. John Downing and Bill Blakely turned up one day at the *Daily Express* office, insisting on taking me out for a celebratory bottle or two of champagne. They told me I'd been responsible for saving their lives.

I never saw Bill again, but John Downing was brought to London as a guest on the TV programme 'This is Your Life' when I was the subject in 1976. Both men have since died.

9

Vietnam

It was one of those nondescript English February mornings, not cold, just dull and overcast. Yet that day is still vividly etched in my mind's eye. I was scared stiff. It was 1968. In faraway Vietnam the Tet offensive was at its height, and I was about to fly out there for the first time.

That morning I took a look around my garden – something I always do when I'm off to any of the world's trouble-spots. The first spring flowers were beginning to push their way through and I was reminded of family lunches out under the apple trees in the summertime. But that day I truly believed I'd never see another English summer.

'Please, God. Let me come home again,' I prayed.

June called me in as it was almost time to leave. Sally gave me a lucky mascot which she'd made from one of her old socks stuffed with rags, with some simple stitching for the eyes and mouth. She told me it was a snake.

'It'll keep you safe, Daddy,' she said, as I tucked it carefully inside my camera-bag.

Then I left the house with a terrible feeling of impending doom and was convinced that I'd be killed in Vietnam.

Approximately 24 hours later I arrived at Saigon's Tan Son Nhut airport on board a giant USAF transporter plane, as there'd been no civil air flights available from Bangkok. The pilot told us we'd just missed a rocket attack on Tan Son Nhut.

As I stepped down onto the tarmac I could literally smell the war – a pungent mixture of heat and aircraft fuel. There were war planes in the air and on the ground, sheltered behind bunkers. A large military ambulance was backing up to one of the transporter planes to transfer its load of wounded soldiers who were being flown to hospitals outside the war-zone.

At the Customs point I had my first experience of the corruption that ruled Saigon, when an official boldly informed me that my films were unlikely to get through. I slipped him two rolls of 35 mm and 40 cigarettes and he let me pass without further trouble.

There were guns everywhere around the hot, dirty airport and many GIs in steel helmets and flak-jackets. It took me two hours to find a taxi to take me to the Caravelle Hotel, the main base for newspapermen in Saigon.

The military presence was abundantly obvious in the streets of the city, but what amazed me was the sight of literally hundreds of motor-scooters darting in and out of the traffic, some carrying two or three extra passengers. With so many people crowding the once elegant boulevards, Saigon reminded me of a seething ant colony.

At the Caravelle I was briefed on the current situation by *Daily Express* correspondent Dennis Blewett. His room was stocked with American 'C' rations (consisting mainly of tinned food to be warmed up on heat blocks in the field), a flak-jacket was slung over a chair and a steel helmet lay on the bed.

'You'll need to get yourself some of that stuff,' said Dennis. 'But first get your accreditation from the American and South Vietnamese Forces.'

He then suggested that I make my way north to Danang and link up with my old friend Stephen Harper who was covering certain battles there.

'Oh, and don't forget to get a bubonic plague jab,' he said, as I was about to leave.

I thought he was joking. Apparently he was not, for the disease was still prevalent in certain rat-infested villages to the north of Saigon. And so I was duly inoculated.

That evening I dined at the Caravelle with several friends whom I'd not seen since the Six Day War in the Middle East. After the meal we stood, sipping gin and tonic, on the hotel roof and watched the war as it raged around the city. Tracer bullets described vivid lines and arcs across the sky, and the glow of hundreds of parachute flares, dropped by USAF planes, could be seen for miles. Out in the suburbs we could see helicopter gunships attacking Viet Cong positions. A long, low rumble came from the distance and someone told me it was the sound of a mass bombing raid by giant B-52 bombers. It was like watching some gigantic, elaborate and sinister cabaret.

Next morning, wearing newly acquired combat gear, I flew up to Danang Air Force base in the company of a troop of fresh-faced young GIs, obviously new to Vietnam. In contrast, at Danang, I saw a group of soldiers who had just returned from the front-line. They were tired, almost numbed, and their helmets and flak-jackets were covered in a kind of red dust. Where they had come from or where they were heading, I never asked. They simply stared into space, completely oblivious to the almost deafening noise of Phantom jets taking off behind them. I wondered how long it would be before my young travelling companions wore those same vacant expressions. How many of them would come out alive?

The Danang Press Centre, run by Marines, was situated downtown, next to a German hospital-ship. On one of the administration huts I noticed a sign commemorating Dickie Chappelle, an old American friend of mine, whom I'd met on an assignment in India. (Dickie had been a great photographer, a respected journalist and a lovely person, one of the few female correspondents to venture into the world's trouble-spots. Sadly she paid the price for her daring for she was killed when she stepped on a land-mine.)

The Marine sergeant in charge of the Press Centre was brisk and efficient as he briefed me on the northern operations. He told me to grab a bed in one of the rooms: 'It's not the Ritz, but it's home,' he said, explaining that the building had housed a brothel during the days of the French.

In fact, the Press Centre proved to be very comfortable with a good bar and restaurant where later that day I met up with Steve Harper. Steve had just returned from covering the besieged US Marine base at Khe Sanh: 'Avoid it if you can,' he advised. Several photographers came in. They sat around telling tales of the front-line which scared the shit out of me. From them I learned that the best action was currently to be found in Hue. 'There's a real ding-dong battle going on up there in and around the Citadel,' said someone. 'Book yourself on one of the military flights up to Phu Bai.'

Before flying on next day I was given a steel helmet and a flak-jacket by a journalist who told me he'd got them from a pile taken from dead and wounded GIs. Steve and I flew combat-fashion (no seats), on board a

C-130 into Phu Bai.

The mud there was ankle-deep and heavy clouds hung low across the sky preventing adequate US air-cover for the men on the ground. We waited with several other journalists, in pouring rain, on a road outside the base, for a convoy heading for Hue. The last convoy had been attacked and two soldiers had been killed, so ours was a nerve-racking ride. We crouched behind the metal sides of the truck for protection as it ploughed its way along rain-sodden roads. The young soldiers with us, nervously pointing their rifles across the rice fields, were covered in the same red dust I'd seen on their comrades the day before.

We discovered Hue to be a small city straddling the Perfume river, to the north of which were the NVA (North Vietnamese Army). Buildings lay in ruins on the outskirts of the city, and we could hear the sounds of a ferocious battle about a mile away. We came to the main bridge across the river, but it had been destroyed, preventing us from going any farther. A long trail of refugees were clambering across the

Injured US Marine, Hue, 1968

broken bridge from the north, reminding me of a similar scene at the Allenby Bridge in Jordan during the Six Day War. Bullets whistled through the air as we made our way to the US command post on the south side of the river.

Steve decided to return to Danang to file his story about the broken bridge while I stayed on hoping to get across the river to join the Marines in the Citadel area. Meanwhile I wandered around the streets of Hue, where I came across a man standing in the rain in what had once been his front-garden. There were five mounds of earth in the garden and they were obviously graves. Choking back his emotions, he told me, in broken English, that they were the graves of his five daughters who had been killed when a shell hit the house. His wife had been so overcome with grief at the loss of her children that she'd gone berserk and had run off into the streets. The man hadn't seen her since.

I stayed overnight at the US command post and listened to the continuous noise of the gunfire outside. During the night I began to feel ill and had several embarrassing bouts of diarrhoea. I also noticed that the plague-jab on my arm was beginning to turn septic so I asked a medic to take a look at it. He told me that I had been injected with a dirty needle, and advised me to try to get some rest. Using my camera-bag as a pillow I tried to follow his advice. I was feverish throughout the night and kept drifting in and out of sleep and thinking about Sally's 'snake' still inside the bag. It must have seen me through because by morning I felt fit again and the injection seemed to be healing up.

Later that morning I managed to get on board a South Vietnamese helicopter piloted by a very brave young man, who made a daring dash across the Perfume river as tracers raced up at us. We landed in a field beside the Citadel where the medics had taken over a small building for use as a casualty station. Several dead bodies lay nearby on stretchers. Some were uncovered, with the rain falling onto their faces; others were already wrapped in body bags waiting to be shipped out.

I rode the short distance to the front-line in a truck which had brought in some of the bodies. There were a couple of young Marines with me.

'Christ! I never knew it would be like this,' said one of them. He saw my cameras. 'You must be crazy, coming here when you don't have to.'

As we edged further forward we crouched lower in the truck for protection. It was then I noticed blood on the floor. I made some remark about it.

'Say, you're English,' said the other Marine. 'Have you ever met the Beatles?'

'Christ!' I thought. 'Here we are kneeling in a pool of blood and shit, and some joker wants to talk about the Beatles!' I told him I'd never met the group. He seemed disappointed and sank back into his own thoughts. We got off the truck near the front.

To get close to the action it was necessary to make an almost suicidal dash down long, narrow streets out of which might come a rocket or machine-gun burst that made you run that much faster. One black soldier was hit in the back of his head by rocket fragmentation, taking this same route. The medics dragged him back and laid him among some boxes of 'C' rations where they proceeded to fight for his life. I never knew whether he lived or died.

Later that day I flew out of Hue on a helicopter carrying dead Marines, some in those morbid body bags, others just piled into the chopper looking as if they were asleep but with their arms and legs sticking out at grotesque angles. Several wounded men were propped up on top of the bodies. An injured black Marine was crying. But, as the helicopter ran the gauntlet out of the Citadel we were all grateful for the extra protection afforded by the cushions of bodies as the NVA fired up at us.

Back in Danang, feeling tired and exhausted, I sent my first pictures of the war in Vietnam back to the *Daily Express*.

Tears of a soldier, Hue, 1968

Next day, Sunday, I was to do it all again with Steve Harper. This time our helicopter had barely reached tree-top height when we were fired upon. A couple of rounds came up through the floor and passed out through the roof, narrowly missing a TV cameraman en route. Luckily the helicopter was undamaged and we were able to fly on and eventually land beside the Citadel once more.

We made our way to a forward command post where we were held up by particularly heavy fighting. While we were waiting there, a sniper was shot out of a nearby palm tree. It happened so quickly that I was unable to raise my camera before his body crashed to the ground.

The body of a Marine padre who'd been hit in the chest was brought in. A Marine chaplain, Eli Takesian, took the body and laid it gently on our truck for the return journey to the heli-pad, during which he shielded an injured and frightened marine.

Back at the casualty station a soldier was cursing the helicopter pilots for not coming in but he didn't realize that would have been suicidal with all the flak that was in the air. I saw the young Marine who had asked me about the Beatles. He looked exhausted but he recognized me instantly.

'I see you're back again, mother fucker!' he said affectionately.

There were more dead bodies outside the hut, some in body bags and others on stretchers, beneath blankets. The place was littered with rounds of live ammunition, rifles, blood-soaked helmets and flak-jackets. A Marine was taking down personal details from the identity tags on the bodies.

'Sorry, fellows,' said a sergeant. 'But there'll be no more choppers coming in

Holy Communion inside a US casualty station, Hue, 1968

today. There's too much shit flying and the clouds are low. You'll have to spend the night here.'

They gave us some 'C' rations and said we could sleep inside the hut so we moved in with the wounded. Someone brought in a couple of stretchers from outside: 'The poor bastards out there won't be needing them,' he said. 'Make yourselves comfortable.'

We warmed up our rations on heat-blocks and despite all the death and destruction, and the sound of war raging outside, I ate hungrily.

It grew dark inside the hut and some candles were lit on a table used by the medics. The candlelight fell only upon the faces of the men grouped around it, while everything else fell off into the shadows. Father Eli offered Holy Communion from a chalice. The scene looked like a Rembrandt painting and photographing it, as one young Marine prayed as I've never seen anyone pray before, I was reminded of childhood Sundays with my grandfather in the small chapel in Oving.

It was midday on Monday when the first helicopter came in to carry off the wounded. Another came in shortly afterwards to collect the dead. I helped to lift on board the body of a skinny young Marine, stiff in rigor mortis and covered with a blanket. The wind from the helicopter rotor blades blew the blanket off his face – he looked like some innocent kid taking a nap. I pictured the heart-break of his mother back home in America. On the journey his stiffened leg kept touching mine until I eventually got cramp in my own leg through trying to avoid the contact. Somehow I couldn't believe that he was dead.

Another day I was sitting combat fashion on the floor of a C-130, waiting to take off on a flight from Phu Bai to Danang. I was thinking about the awful things I'd seen in the previous few days and reflecting that my own skin and clothes were now ingrained with the red dust of Vietnam. (In fact the only things distinguishing me from the soldiers were the cameras that hung constantly around my neck ready for use at a moment's notice.) As I sat there, lost in my own thoughts, there was a commotion at the door and a welfare worker appeared with several small children – I learned later that they had all been orphaned by the war. One by one she lifted them onto the plane and sat them between our legs. One little girl, with long black hair and a beautiful face, clung onto me. Big tears rolled down her cheeks as we took off. She hardly moved throughout the flight and must have been bewildered by what was happening to her. When we landed and she was taken off by the woman, the little girl gave me the merest flicker of a smile. That night I wrote to June telling her about the girl and the compassion I had felt for her. Like a lot of other western journalists who found themselves in the same situation, I felt that I wanted to adopt one of these beautiful children and give them some of the security enjoyed by my own family.

Feeling tired and emotionally drained I decided to try and relax for a day or two in Saigon. I spent most of this time sitting with other correspondents at the veranda bar of the Continental (the hotel featured in Graham Greene's classic novel *The Quiet American*), where, under huge rotating fans, we were served gin and tonics by waiters who looked as old as the elegant building itself. We watched Saigon go by: the GIs, the overloaded motor-scooters, the military hardware and the dainty girls with their colourful silken dresses which were slit to the waist and worn over elegant trousers. There were good restaurants in Saigon, good tailors, bath-houses and massage parlours. I quickly learned that it was possible to buy almost anything in the city. You name it – Saigon could supply it.

There were various battles I had to cover in other parts of the country, including some time spent with an Australian unit in the

Overleaf
A father carries his children through the battered streets during a lull in the fighting, Hue, 1968

south. But towards the end of March I returned to Danang to cover more operations in the north.

In the Danang Press Centre I met up with my old friend Larry Burrows, who now spent most of his time covering the Vietnam war for *Life* magazine. We had a reunion dinner together and discussed the possibility of getting into Khe Sanh where 3,000 US Marines were still pinned down by the NVA.

After a couple of abortive attempts at getting there, we eventually found ourselves with three other newsmen on board a rather battered Marine helicopter, flying alongside another craft which was equipped with better navigational aids. Our destination was a forward base called Stud, on Highway 9, from where the operation to relieve Khe Sanh was to be launched. Things went well for the first hour, then we flew into a patch of dense cloud, losing sight of the accompanying helicopter. Our craft seemed to fumble around for a while, unable to find its direction. The emergency alarms started up and a worried crewman wearing a life-jacket came back. He told us to remove our helmets and flak-jackets and don life-jackets as quickly as possible. We were fast running out of fuel over territory then held by the North Vietnamese. If we put down there we stood every chance of being captured by 'Charlie' (nickname for North Vietnamese Communist forces). To avoid this horrifying fate we were heading out to sea. The crewman told us to inflate our life-jackets just enough for buoyancy as a fully inflated jacket would not pass through the door. He added that the helicopter was likely to plunge at least 20 feet below the surface before the rotor-blades stopped spinning, only then would we be able to bale out!

Amid the noise and confusion I tried to blow some air into my life-jacket, but nothing happened. 'Just my bloody luck,' I thought. 'I've picked a dud one!' Perhaps this was the dreadful end I'd been worried about in my garden back home. I fumbled with the jacket a bit more and discovered that I hadn't pulled down a plastic cover on the nozzle. I yanked at it and blew again.

Thankfully, the jacket began to grow.

Then the sea came up through the mist about 30 feet below. We were almost skimming the waves when the pilot straightened out. Two rescue choppers came out to find us and then escorted us to Quang Tri airbase. It felt good to be back on dry land. Later that day Larry and I were airborne again in the same helicopter. This time we made it to Stud.

Many helicopters were to-ing and fro-ing across the sky at Stud as they prepared for the next day's operation which was to be the biggest heli-borne assault ever mounted, involving something like 450 machines.

Things grew quiet at Stud, save for the occasional incoming rocket, as night came in and we were able to leave our cameras in a Press tent while we took a bath, under guard, in a nearby water-hole. It wasn't exactly the Caravelle Hotel, but it was good to be able to wash away the troubles of the day.

In the morning, men of the Air Cavalry formed up in groups and troops with their faces blackened were loaded up with weapons and ammunition. Their commander, General Tolson, came to give them a pep talk and the scene was reminiscent of newsreel films I'd seen of preparations for the D-Day landings in Normandy. Someone told me that the Air Cavalry were the modern version of the unit once commanded by General Custer.

'Let's hope it won't be another Little Big Horn,' I remarked to Larry.

He and I were to ride in the command heicopter, a Huey, with Colonel Sweet. Hueys are often used open-sided in combat, so we had a clear view of the shell-scarred landscape around Khe Sanh. Up ahead we saw the smoke of an artillery barrage, followed by bombing and strafing by US fighter-planes as they prepared the way for our arrival on Hill Timothy. The helicopters looked like a plague of locusts descending as we went down in the tall elephant grass.

We jumped down and the helicopters rose again, very quickly. Unfortunately, the strap of my water-bottle got hooked up on

Dug-out on Hill Timothy, 1968

part of the superstructure and I began to rise again! For a few agonizing seconds I hung in mid-air like a helpless puppet. Luckily the strap snapped at about five feet and I fell unharmed into the grass.

The noise of the helicopters soon faded into the distance and for a short while the only sound came from the cool breeze as it blew lazily against the tall grass. But the area was soon secured and buzzing with activity. Then more helicopters came in with yet more troops.

That night several soldiers were killed and others wounded by incoming rockets on nearby Hill Tom. Next morning, as our positions were reinforced with artillery pieces flown in by helicopter, Larry and I dug a shallow trench near the command bunker, for our own protection.

There were many North Vietnamese in the surrounding hills and consequently the air-strikes continued throughout the day. There were clouds of smoke in every direction, and the surrounding terrain, pock-marked by shell-holes and bomb-craters, began to resemble the surface of the moon.

As evening approached, some hot food was flown in (the Air Cavalry really knew how to look after their men in the field). I was about to take my first mouthful when a rocket landed with a tremendous crash about 20 yards away. Forgetting the food I dived headlong into a large dug-out shelter as more rounds landed. An artillery officer was hit in the back by a piece of shrapnel. Luckily, the thickness of his flak-jacket saved his life and he escaped with bad bruising.

As darkness fell I joined Larry in our trench. We were very uncomfortable as we lay side by side listening to the noise of the shelling and realized that the trench was too short, too narrow and not deep enough for our proper protection. It started to rain during the night and I managed only a fitful sleep from which I awoke at daybreak, cold, damp and miserable.

The hillside was quiet and still and the rain had turned to fog. The stench of war hung unmistakably on the early morning air. Dead bodies lay nearby, already wrapped in the all-too-familiar body bags waiting, ready to be shipped out for burial. They were the results of the night's shelling and rocket fire. A few shadowy figures moved about in the mist.

I saw a couple of wounded men waiting to be Medivaced out. I realized that the victims might easily have been me. Suddenly I felt very lonely. I wanted to go home – to be with June and Jayne, Sally and Lucy. I wondered what they would be doing that day and wondered if I would ever see them again.

The air filled with the noise of helicopters coming in to evacuate the wounded and carry off the dead. As I watched them coming down through the pale light I remember thinking: 'Should I jump aboard and get away from all this danger?' I kept watching until the evacuation was completed and kept thinking about running, but I didn't move. One by one the helicopters took off again until they had all gone and the silence had returned.

That day Larry and I dug the trench deeper, longer and wider. We even put in some shelves made from old boxes, on which to keep our cameras. We pulled our poncho groundsheets across the trench to keep out the rain and I put up a sign saying 'Hotel Timothy – Press Centre'.

That evening, as dusk approached, Larry and I sat on the hillside overlooking Khe Sanh. We were joined by a US Army padre who apologized for his intrusion but explained that he felt like company. He was about 30 years old and for some reason carried two copies of the Bible. He told us that he'd only been with the Air Cavalry for a couple of weeks and this was his first experience of war. The three of us talked, our voices growing softer and softer as the darkness engulfed us. We talked of our lives back home, our families and the fears I had experienced that morning. I reasoned why I hadn't run for the helicopters: you don't run from an assignment until it's finished to the best of your ability, no matter how scared you might be. You don't take the easy way out. Larry agreed that this was so. He, too, understood the code.

By 9 o'clock Larry and I were back in our trench. It was pitch-black and the rockets and shells were coming in thick and fast, landing even closer than the previous night. I tried to sleep through all the noise, covering my face with my steel helmet, but it was impossible.

At one point I scrambled over to the command post to find out what was going on. I tripped over something and fell head-first into a dug-out among the Colonel and his men whose faces were lit by dim light. I decided against asking any questions and scrambled back to our trench as more shells were coming in, their vibration causing the dirt to crumble and fall in off the walls of the trench.

There was a large can of coffee brewing nearby next morning, from which we filled our mess-tins. It tasted good, although under other circumstances I'd have sworn that someone had thrown their old socks in it. Drinking it with Larry I asked him what we should do that day.

He looked up at the dark, brooding sky: 'Exposure one second, aperture 2.8,' he said with a grin.

Later that day we were air-lifted off Hill Timothy and taken to Hill 471 which overlooked the devastated town of Khe Sanh on one side and the besieged Marine base, in the distance, on the other. Some 'Charlies' (either very brave or drugged up to the eyeballs), who had tried to storm the hill during the night were lying dead on the barbed wire fence farther down the hill. The sweet,

Larry Burrows and I in our trench on Hill Timothy, 1968

120

sickly smell of bodies decomposing in the sun hung in the air.

We decided to dig in again but, pushing a spade into the ground, I hit the soft remains of a North Vietmanese soldier and we moved away, reluctant to try elsewhere.

We spent that night sitting upright in a cramped dug-out with some GIs. We were expecting the usual attack, but it turned out to be a relatively quiet night and I was able to grab some sleep.

I had by now been 'out' for five days – a long time for a daily newspaperman to be out of touch with his office. My material was 'perishable' and I told Larry that I'd get on board the next available flight back to Danang. He had no deadline to meet and decided to stay on. He gave me a package of films to take back to Saigon for eventual shipment to the States.

As I sat there writing my captions, I surveyed the scene around me. Tired soldiers were cleaning their guns and drying their clothes in the sun. Huge dewdrops hung on the barbed-wire. I looked at the bodies of the North Vietnamese hanging on the fence, and beyond them, the ruined town of Khe Sanh. It was at this exact moment that Larry came over to tell me that Martin Luther King had been assassinated in Memphis – one of the GIs had picked up the news on his transistor radio and for a while we all forgot about the war.

But it was soon back to the present reality. Larry was moving out with a patrol. We shook hands and I watched them move off in single file through a gap in the wire. They walked gingerly across a minefield with about 20 yards between each man, then they disappeared over a ridge in the distance.

I flew back to London on Easter week-end, having been in Vietnam for ten weeks, and considered myself lucky to be alive. I travelled first-class from Singapore, drinking a few glasses of champagne en route. I'd promised myself this luxury during 'silly talk' with some of the Marines back in Hue.

There were some copies of the *Daily Express* on board the plane with a half-page

'Fincher File' showing some of my pictures from Hill Timothy. On the facing page were details of a big anti-Vietnam demonstration to be held in London on Easter Monday. This news and the champagne brought my emotions to the surface. Other passengers eyed me suspiciously as I sat there silently toasting the brave young men stuck on the hillsides of Vietnam. I knew I had to cover that demonstration.

On Easter Monday I went to Grosvenor Square, where the march ended in violence outside the US Embassy. I saw the contorted faces of the demonstrators and I was angry; it took a lot of self-control not to get involved. I wondered what those people would have said to the man in Hue with the burial mounds in his garden, or the little girl on the helicopter, or any of the young GIs covered in red mud, or the parents whose sons ended up in body bags . . .

I wanted to tell them that newspapermen like myself were not allowed into North Vietnam to see thing from the Communist side – it was a closed shop. I believe a few Western correspondents did manage to get

Together with my family after returning from Vietnam, Easter, 1968

into Hanoi at one stage of the war, but they were given little more than a guided tour. Surely the freedom of movement I had been given by the Americans was what it was all about?

Those people were claiming to understand the world's problems.

I'll never understand them.

Almost six months later, in October, I was in my garden again, taking my ritual look at some of the things I love. The colours of the dahlias seemed exaggerated in the afternoon light. The soil, as I turned it, smelled good and earthy. Mr Kemp, a retired gardener who lives in the village, stopped by to give me some advice on my roses, something like, 'Remember, three buds up,' he said. I wasn't paying much attention as I was due to leave for Vietnam the next day, and once again I was scared stiff.

This time I was flying out with Lieut-Colonel Colin Mitchell – 'Mad Mitch' of the Aden days. Colin had left the army by then and had been commissioned by the *Daily Express* to write some special features on the Vietnam war.

Soon after booking into the Continental Palace, Colin told me that he'd brought along his old service revolver.

'But newspapermen don't carry arms,' I said.

A few days later I learned that he'd disposed of the gun, piece by piece, down the drains of the city!

The northern area of South Vietnam was still the most newsworthy and I soon found myself back at the Danang Press Centre. Our first assignment was to pay a very brief visit to a Marine unit which was preparing to relieve a besieged Special Forces (Green Berets) camp at Thong Duc. The Marines were encamped on Hill 682, some 2,000 ft, above the Song Vugoi river, where they had cleared a helicopter landing-space in the bamboo forest. We went in on a re-supply helicopter flown by a very nervous crew, for a few helicopters had already been shot down in the area during the past week.

Our plan was to stay for just 20 minutes, but as the helicopter took off again it attracted heavy NVA fire and was unable to return to pick us up. We were left with no alternative but to make ourselves comfortable. We sat on upturned boxes in the jungle clearing talking and brewing up with some tea-bags I'd brought from England. As darkness engulfed us, the jungle came alive with noises and fire-flies flitted around like miniature, illuminated helicopters. Then a flare-ship flew over, dropping flares which lit up the night sky.

I went to sleep at 9 o'clock stretched out on the ground with my poncho ground-sheet strung up in the trees above me, quite oblivious to the presence of the snakes and scorpions which inhabited the area.

The monsoon broke at midnight, its noise drumming on the groundsheet and the leaves above me. But I was secure and dry beneath the poncho and managed to sleep a little. By dawn, however, the rain was at full pelt and I had to dig a small trench around my dry patch to divert the water that was trickling towards me. It made little difference and I was soon drenched to the skin.

To get up to this position Colonel Nielson and his 800 Marines had been on the move for eight days, carrying all their supplies including 41-mm mortars and ammunition and until the previous night had to carry all their water – now they were awash with the stuff!

It was midday before we moved off towards the Green Berets' camp, slipping and sliding through the wet jungle and wading waist-deep through a river and paddy fields. Red blobs began to appear on the trousers of some of the Marines. Pulling them down they found leeches clinging to them, grown fat on their blood. They quickly burned the sluglike creatures off with cigarettes.

We came under some small-arms fire as we approached the Special Forces Camp, but arrived in the compound there without casualties. Colin and I were stuck there for five days, throughout which my clothes remained soaking wet, although I did manage to keep my cameras reasonably dry in a waterproof pack.

One morning the Marines decided to push across the swollen river in search of the enemy. As they moved off, a salvo of shells fell on a nearby village killing and wounding several inhabitants. I never knew which side fired the shells but it really upset a certain group of Special Forces men who had been working with the villagers, teaching them new agricultural methods and some elementary engineering and even, on one or two occasions, delivering babies! Colin and I watched these men doing everything that was humanly possible as they now tried to save lives in the village.

On the fifth day the clouds began to lift, although it was still raining. The occasional helicopter passed high overhead but they were reluctant to come down as they would invariably be shot at by the NVA.

'You'll have to pop some smoke [a hand-grenade that produced a coloured smoke] to get one down,' said a Marine on duty at the heli-pad.

By this time Colin and I were getting desperate to despatch our story and pictures and we were glad when someone did 'pop some bright orange smoke'. In no time at all a chopper came down looking for a Medivac case. As the tail-door dropped Colin and I scrambled aboard with our conducting officer. The crewman made it quite clear that he didn't want us aboard and the helicopter put down again after only a ten-minute flight. The crewman tried to con us into believing that we'd arrived in Danang. Of course we knew this wasn't true and refused to get off so he was forced to take us all the way to Danang. I still find it unbelievable that these men were willing to play 'silly buggers' in the midst of a war.

Colin Mitchell had now covered his first major assignment. While I believe he had always understood the difficulties faced by newspapermen in the field, I was none the less amazed by his rapid transition from soldier to correspondent. His reporting could not be faulted and he sent back several first-class articles from Vietnam.

It was during this time that I went on a helicopter assault with a battalion of the 21st Infantry near Tay Ninh. During the assault a message came through that an armed US helicopter had been shot down over the jungle. They had managed to get down all right, the crew were still alive and we were to go in and mount a rescue operation.

Our helicopter went down in a clearing while others covered us with machine-gun fire and a smoke-screen. As we landed the Viet Cong opened fire but luckily no one was hit and we ran towards the elephant grass surrounding the clearing. It was a mile walk into the jungle from there, before we would reach the men. The first stretch was safe enough because of the camouflage afforded by the tall grass. But, once we entered the jungle itself, we became a clear target for 'Charlie', who we knew was there watching us from somewhere behind the foliage.

The heat became more intense as we walked deeper into the dark trees. We saw old tin-cans and footprints leading off into the jungle. The stench of stale urine hung on the air, assaulting the nostrils with every intake of breath. To make matters worse I had begun to dehydrate. My mouth was as dry as cardboard and the camera straps seemed to be cutting deep into my neck. I felt sick and scared.

The soldiers with me were every bit as nervous as me. They peered into the dark-green density of the jungle as they edged stealthily forward and every so often the awful quietness was disturbed by a cracking twig or the cursing of a disgruntled soldier.

We reached the men, who were sheltering in an old bomb-crater, with their helicopter lying wrecked nearby. Our Captain quickly checked over the helicopter, set fire to it and then got us moving again on the long walk back to the rescue helicopter. The tension was unbearable as we retraced our steps and waited for the inevitable attack from the trees. I felt sure I'd collapse before we reached the clearing, but somehow I managed to keep going. Perhaps fear was the spur.

The moment we reached the elephant grass 'Charlie' opened fire on us, with everything he'd got. The US gunships were firing too, from above, to give us cover. I saw our helicopter coming in up ahead. I ran like hell towards it and leapt on board, collapsing on the deck with the hair standing up on the back of my neck. As we rose, agonizingly slowly, out of the clearing a couple of bullets ripped through the fuselage. But we still rose. When we were safely out of danger I sat with my legs dangling out of the door, gulping in the cold air and beginning to feel better already.

I revisited Hue, and out of curiosity went to see the house where I'd met the man who had lost his five daughters and whose wife had run off in despair. The house was reduced to an empty shell and the burial mounds had completely disappeared, probably washed away by the monsoon. I have often wondered what became of the man.

On another occasion in Hue I was invited to a small school-house a few miles outside the city where some gruesome reminders of the Tet offensive were on display. These were the skeletal remains of some 500 slaughtered victims during the North Vietnamese purge of the northern part of Hue. At the height of the offensive these people had been roped together and marched out to this lonely spot where they had been

South Vietnamese Ranger launches an attack on a Viet Cong bunker

Overleaf   The attack continues: some are hurt; some are killed. Comrades recover bodies

executed. Some of the bones were still roped together and some of the skulls had been shattered by blows, while others bore single bullet-holes. Relatives of the victims were searching among a pile of documents and clothes for positive identification of their loved ones. They searched in a silence which was occasionally broken by a piercing cry of recognition.

One evening late in 1970, over a meal in a small restaurant just around the corner from the Caravelle Hotel in Saigon, I said yet another farewell to Larry Burrows. (I remember that he recommended the asparagus!) Needless to say most of the conversation revolved around photography. Out in the street we shook hands and looked forward to our next meeting, although neither of us had any idea when this would be. I was bound for London next morning and Larry was off to cover some new area of the war in Vietnam.

In February 1971 I was at Waterloo Station in London, about to catch an early even-

126

ing train home when a loudspeaker announcement asked me to go to the station master's office. Awaiting me there was a telephone call from a London TV station. A voice bluntly asked me 'Have you heard about Larry Burrows?'

I wasn't exactly sure what they were talking about and I was shocked when they explained that Larry had been on board a South Vietnamese helicopter which had been shot down over the jungle in Laos. I found it difficult to believe that he was dead. Of all the brave photographers I'd known in Vietnam, Larry Burrows was the one I'd thought most likely to survive. He had more

confidence in his own sense of infallibility than anyone else I'd known.

I made my way aimlessly through the home-going crowds in the station. I watched prospective customers riffling through the pages of the newspapers and magazines in the news-stall in the centre of the station, and I wondered how many of them realized the hard work and the heartbreak that went into producing their entertainment.

My last visit to Vietnam came in 1975 just before the fall of Xuan Loc, a town which lies 70 miles to the east of Saigon. Many

Australians and Viet Cong prisoner, 1969

towns, including Danang, had already fallen to the Communists. The Americans had long since withdrawn and the South Vietnamese Forces were gamely holding out against impossible odds.

It was now an entirely different situation for newspapermen covering the remains of the war. The elaborate press facilities, flak-jackets, steel helmets and helicopter rides to the front-line, had all gone with the departure of the Americans. We were more or less on our own.

It was impossible to get into Xuan Loc by road, or so I discovered when sharing a taxi with a team from the *Sunday Times*. We got pinned down by mortar-fire near the front. Our driver, lying beside us in the ditch, must have wondered what sort of a tip he'd be getting. He refused to try again next day.

I eventually managed to get on board a South Vietnamese helicopter, which was flying a party of 25 journalists into Xuan Loc. So, too, did Stephen Harper who was back in Vietnam to cover the final days for the *Daily Express*. I felt virtually naked without a flak-jacket or helmet and the flight itself did little to settle my nerves, for we flew literally at tree-top level, in order to avoid the North Vietnamese rockets.

We put down safely on a road beside a banana plantation, where other helicopters were re-supplying the South Vietnamese Forces and Medivacing the wounded out. Clouds of the familiar red dust blew everywhere amid the commotion.

We drove into the devastated town on a truck commandeered by our conducting officer, an immaculately dressed South Vietnamese Special Forces Captain. Tin roofs lay dented and bent in the street and buildings were burning everywhere. Miraculously, as we drove deeper into the town towards the South Vietnamese HQ, the NVA stopped firing.

A number of NVA prisoners were tied up and blindfolded and sitting in the dirt at the headquarters. Their heads twisted and turned in anxious anticipation as I walked around them looking for the best angle for photography.

Next Steve and I made a dash across an open field to where some paratroopers were holding the perimeter. One of them showed us a dent in his steel helmet: he'd been shot at while making the same dash across the same field!

After a while we made it back to the banana plantation where in the middle of clouds of swirling red dust, hundreds of people were trying to scramble onto the helicopters while medics were trying to load the wounded on board. The conducting officer, a radio reporter and I somehow got separated from Steve and the rest of the journalists. The conducting officer told us that our helicopter was about to come in and that we *must* get aboard quickly, otherwise we were likely to be left in Xuan Loc until the North Vietnamese arrived. I looked around again for Steve and the others but they were nowhere to be seen. By now the conducting officer and the radio reporter were on board and beckoning furiously to me to join them. I threw my cameras up to the officer, then started to help a family into the craft.

The rear tail-ramp was already going up, preventing some children from getting on board. The Special Forces Captain was holding his rifle threateningly over the crowd, as he didn't want the craft to overload. I got caught up in a bicycle frame which an old man was trying to heave aboard. I cursed the man but somehow got myself untangled and was able to pull another youngster on board with me.

The helicopter began to rise. Ten feet. Twenty feet. Thirty feet. That's when I saw a little girl – clinging on for all she was worth to the superstructure. There was no way I could reach her. Suddenly she disappeared. Her mother was already on board with three or four other children and she tried to jump off after her daughter, but some other refugees managed to pull her back. After that she just sat there on the floor of the helicopter, crying her heart out. It was awful to watch her grief, but there was little anyone could do to comfort her. I felt guilty –

Overleaf
House of Death, Hue, 1969

perhaps I should have stayed on the ground and pushed more kids onto the helicopter. As we flew on I took out my camera and, though it sounds mercenary, I began taking pictures of the woman. I had to do something to hide my feelings.

Weeping mother. Her daughter had fallen from refugee helicopter, Xuan Loc, 1975

'Boat People', Hong Kong, 1979

Next day I was walking along Saigon's Tu Do Street, having just photographed a group of Boy Scouts, Cubs and Girl Guides sitting in a circle on the green outside the Presidential Palace (I later learned that this had been the last-ever meeting of these youngsters in South Vietnam). I had one camera around my neck and two more slung across my shoulder. Suddenly a motor-scooter brushed past me on the pavement. The pillion passenger grabbed the straps on my shoulder and that was the last I ever saw of those cameras. 'Christ! The war is on their doorstep and they're still thieving!' I thought. I was left with just one camera and one lens (my other equipment had been damaged when I had dived for cover in Xuan Loc). Someone suggested that I buy another camera from 'Thieves' Market', a black-market centre where you could often buy back your own stolen equipment for a reasonable price! My own cameras were not there, so I bought a clapped-out looking model which proved to be totally useless.

We were summoned to a press conference at the British Embassy, where the staff were preparing to move out, and told of the emergency plans should the Communists arrive suddenly in Saigon. If we heard Bing Crosby singing 'White Christmas' on the radio then we were to make for a certain building from where we would be evacuated.

After that meeting I sat down and thought things over, reasoning that if I stayed on much longer then I could possibly find myself detained in Vietnam for a very long time. Unlike most of my colleagues I had no large organization to support me. I had my own small business to run back home and could not afford such a delay, added to which was the fact that I was carrying no equipment to speak of. After much deliberation I decided to get out while I could.

I left Tan Son Nhut on a flight bound for Bangkok. Even though I believed that I had made the right decision, inwardly I felt a coward – it was the first time I'd ever turned my back on a war assignment.

I have never been back to Vietnam since then.

Of course the Vietnam story did not end when the war was over. In 1979 the 'Boat People' hit the headlines for a while. Thousands of South Vietnamese refugees were fleeing their country in hundreds of overcrowded boats. Many of these craft were unseaworthy and many people died in their desperate attempt to escape. Many fell prey to Thai pirates who attacked them and stole Vietnamese possessions. And when the Boat People did reach other waters they were often turned away, unwelcome and unwanted.

I covered the exodus at its height. But by then it was difficult to project the full impact of the particular legacy of the Vietnam war to a world increasingly concerned with its own safety and security.

10

Famous Faces

I have met and photographed many famous people from a variety of professions, including those involved in politics, religion, cinema, theatre, music and literature. Some personalities proved to be arrogant and distant. Those I have chosen to forget. Others, however, were helpful, kind, friendly and, above all, human. These I remember with fondness.

Among the most memorable subjects (not only for me but, I'm sure, for many other press photographers, too) was Sir Winston Churchill, whom I first photographed in the early fifties when he paid a visit to a Conservative Club in a South London suburb. Several women (who had, in all probability, voted Labour in the last election) stood goggle-eyed in the street as Churchill passed by. Like them I, too, was mesmerized by the presence of the great man, and I never really lost that sense of awe on the other occasions on which I photographed him.

Just before Christmas 1953, Keystone sent me and Mick Miller – another young photographer – along to Downing Street to photograph Prime Minister Churchill as he left for Chartwell, his country home, where he was to spend the festive season.

'Door-stepping' at Downing Street has never been a very enviable assignment. It is a dimly-lit thoroughfare even in summertime; often, an unpleasant wind blows along its length from St James's Park to Whitehall.

Despite the pouring rain that day, Mick and I arrived early, equipped with the crude cameras of the time and large flash-guns with magnesium bulbs. The black-caped policeman on duty allowed us to position ourselves on either side of the door; that way, we reckoned, at least one of us would get a picture of Churchill. Soon we were joined by several other photographers.

At five o'clock the black front-door opened and a commissionaire stepped out leading Rufus, Sir Winston's pet poodle. Then, the Prime Minister emerged, helped by Lady Churchill. We proffered the season's greeting to the famous couple and asked them to 'Hold it!' They stood on the steps with the end of Sir Winston's cigar no more than a yard from Mick's camera.

Suddenly there was an almighty bang. For a moment I thought a bomb had gone off somewhere nearby, then I realized that Mick's flash-bulb had exploded, showering the Prime Minister's homburg with bits of sizzling glass and cellophane.

Mr Winston Churchill arrives at Westerham Church, Kent, 1952, hand-in-hand with his four-year-old grandson, Nicholas Soames, to attend the christening of Jeremy Soames

Sir Winston removed the cigar slowly from his mouth and his famous voice barked out an order: 'Take that man's name,' he said to his detective. He and Lady Churchill then climbed into a waiting Humber Super Snipe and were driven away towards Whitehall.

Poor old Mick was rather shaken by the unfortunate accident: 'I suppose I'll be spending Christmas in the Bloody Tower,' he said gloomily as we made our way back to Fleet Street. But I don't think he ever heard any more about the incident. Churchill was probably joking.

Early in my career I photographed Sir Winston arriving at a church at Westerham, in Kent, for the christening of one of his grandchildren. On that occasion he wore a very smart checkered suit, a bow-tie and a grey homburg. When I photographed him in the summer of 1962 he was wearing exactly the same clothes he'd worn for the chris-

tening. This time he was returning home to Hyde Park Gate, having spent some weeks in the Middlesex Hospital recovering from an illness.

An enormous crowd of well-wishers had gathered to welcome him in the sunshine outside his home. A pair of ambulancemen lifted him in a wheelchair down onto the pavement and began to carry him towards the house. 'Not feet first,' he commanded. They turned him around to face the crowd. At the top of the steps he lifted his hat in salute and I took my photograph. Then he was gone with the door firmly closed behind him. The old warrior was home again after another battle won.

I have mentioned earlier the long period I spent 'door-stepping' Sir Winston's home in the spring of 1963: it proved to be a well-rewarded wait. One afternoon a Humber, flying the pennant of the Cinque Ports, pulled up at the kerbside. Ed Murray, Churchill's personal detective, stepped out and gave me a knowing wink before disappearing into the house. A few minutes later the great man was helped out of the house and into the car by his secretary, Montague Browne.

Fortunately I had a *Daily Express* despatch rider with me. I jumped on the back of his motor-cycle and we followed the car, through the city traffic, to Richmond Park where it turned into a 'No Entry' road and parked beside a 'Do Not Feed the Animals' notice. Then a hand poked through the window offering a morsel of food to a herd of deer grazing nearby and a couple of animals stepped warily forward.

Sir Winston was then helped out of the car to stand in the pale sunlight feeding the deer with slices of bread from a packet held under his arm. I was about to begin photographing the scene when a Park Ranger rode up on horseback.

'You can't park here,' he said to me authoritatively. He looked at the deer nibbling happily at the bread. 'And feeding the animals is definitely not allowed,' he continued, obviously unaware who the illustrious visitor was.

'You'd better tell him that yourself,' I said.

The Ranger nudged his horse a step nearer the car.

'That,' I said, 'is Sir Winston Churchill.'

The Ranger did a double-take and almost fell off his horse. He said nothing more, but just sat there watching and probably realizing how close he had come to the biggest mistake

Sir Winston Churchill goes back to Harrow, his old school, and gives the 'V' sign to cheering boys

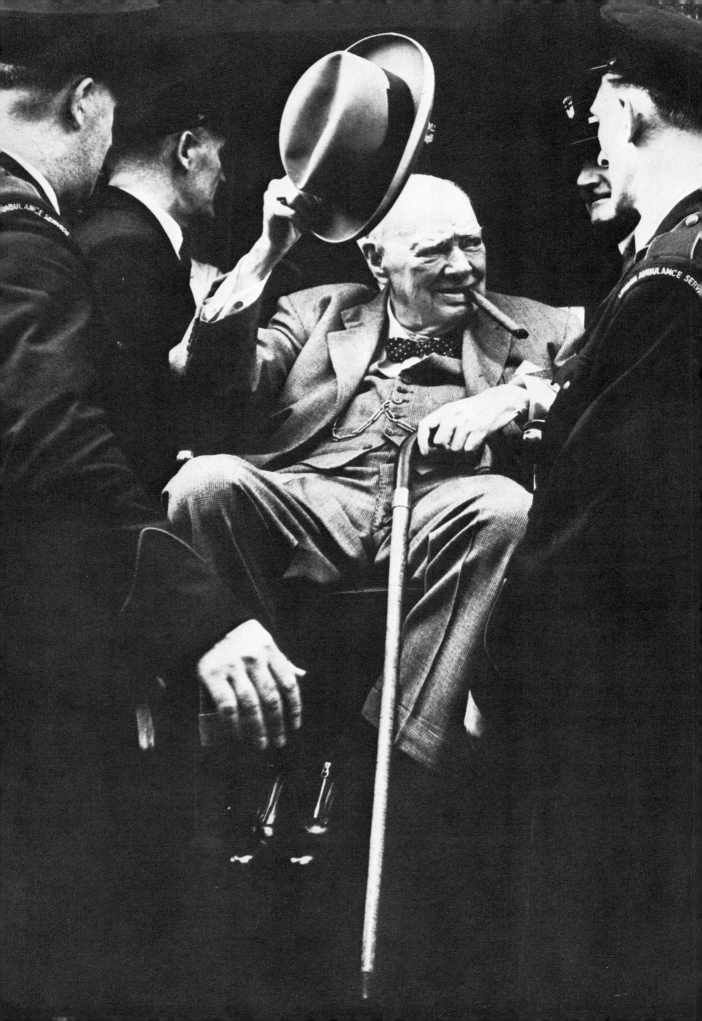

Come on, I won't bite you!

Picture by
TERRY FINCHER

His days of struggle are long past. Now, loaded with years and honour, he stands in the pale sunshine of Richmond Park to feed the deer. And watch spring

The half-page picture of Sir Winston Churchill with deer in Richmond Park as published in the *Daily Express*, 26 March 1963

of his career.

My photograph of the scene must be among the last pictures taken of Sir Winston out and about in his beloved England.

Later that same year I took my final picture of the 'Old Man' when he appeared with Lady Churchill at the window of their home on the occasion of his eighty-ninth birthday.

Sir Winston Churchill died on 24 January 1965. I heard the news while in the company of several correspondents in the Giyon Palace Hotel in Addis Ababa while covering the Royal tour of Ethiopia. A sad silence fell over the group of seasoned journalists clustered around the bar and that night we drank to the memory of one of our greatest subjects.

Another great subject was Nikita Khrushchev, whom I first encountered in April 1956, when he arrived in London on a good-

Sir Winston Churchill is carried into his Hyde Park Gate home on return from hospital in 1962. (He is wearing the same suit that he wore to his grandson's christening in 1952.)

will visit with fellow Russian leader Nikolai Bulganin. I was assigned by Keystone to take only general crowd-scenes but, feeling a great sense of occasion, I became determined to get some pictures of the distinguished visitors. With me I took a 5 × 4 camera and my brand-new electronic flash-unit, which included a huge battery weighing more than 16 lb, and went along to Claridge's Hotel in Mayfair, where the politicians were staying. I diligently parked myself on the pavement outside the hotel – and waited.

An hour or so later, my patience was rewarded when Bulganin and Khrushchev left the hotel for a tour of the sights of London. As their car edged its way through the crowds, I pushed myself forward and, despite a certain amount of aggravation from the security policemen, I found myself only a yard or so from Khrushchev's smiling face. I tapped on his window and he turned towards me. I took the photograph.

I felt that my luck was in for I had Khrushchev 'in the can' now, and all I

needed to complete the set was Bulganin. I looked around in the crowd and saw Ron Dumont, a photographer, frantically waving at me from his car. 'Come on, Terry,' he said. 'Let's follow them!'

Ron had a reputation as a fast driver, so I willingly jumped in beside him. He weaved in and out of the rush-hour traffic, keeping the Russians' car firmly in sight. One very alert policeman spotted our pursuit and, thinking that we might be crazed assassins or something, he leapt in front of the car. Ron swerved expertly and I heard the policeman's tunic brush against the side of the car. I glanced around to see the unharmed but definitely angry constable shaking a fist at us.

Resuming our chase we saw the Russians' car pulling up outside Westminster Abbey. Bulganin and Khrushchev went inside the Abbey to lay a weath at the tomb of the Unknown Warrior. While they were doing this I elbowed my way to their limousine so that I was standing beside the rear windows. A few minutes later Bulganin climbed back in, but despite my frantic tapping on his window he continued to look away from me. Then Khrushchev recognized me from our previous encounter at Claridge's and he pointed me out to his companion. Bulganin turned his smiling face towards me and I took the photograph. The results were pin-sharp and appeared on almost every front page next day.

My next meeting with Khrushchev came in the early sixties when I flew out to Moscow to cover the official visit there by Harold Wilson, then leader of the Labour Party, and the Shadow Foreign Secretary, Patrick Gordon Walker. One day I accompanied Mr Wilson into the Kremlin itself. We, the Press, entered through a small door set in a high wall, then followed an official along a maze of corridors to the ante-room where Wilson was to meet Khrushchev.

Sir Winston and Lady Churchill appear for the crowds at the window of their Hyde Park Gate home on the occasion of his eighty-ninth birthday, 1964. This was the last time Churchill was photographed; he died a few months later

As we were waiting a door at the other end of the room swung open and through it I saw an image that I've never forgotten. Nikita Khrushchev, head bowed in concentration over some documents, was seated at the end of a long conference table bordered by rows of empty chairs. A stern-faced portrait of Lenin hung on the wall behind him. I was about to take a photograph of this moment when the door closed again.

Khrushchev and Wilson had their meeting which I duly photographed. I was nevertheless annoyed at having missed that much more powerful shot earlier.

However, next day a second meeting was scheduled in the same room. Sure enough the same door opened presenting me with the same view. This time I was prepared and I took two quick exposures before the door closed again. (The picture was published in the *Daily Express*, but I was unable to obtain a print of it. Sadly, I heard that the negative was later mislaid in an office clean-up.)

I was in Moscow again in 1964, to cover the signing of the A-bomb Treaty. Accompanying me on this assignment was Roy Dickens, working for *Paris Match*, and we were together, with Khrushchev, in the same room mentioned earlier when the telephone rang. Khrushchev reached out a chubby hand and lifted the receiver to his ear. He listened intently for a while, then a broad smile crossed his face, reminding me more of a friendly uncle than a powerful world leader. He put down the phone and spoke a few words to his interpreter and then the interpreter turned to Roy and me.

'Gentlemen. You have a scoop!' he said and I anxiously wondered if perhaps the Russians had attacked America. But the interpreter continued: 'That was a call from our space centre – we have just launched *another* man successfully into space.'

Khrushchev was still beaming at the good news as he posed for us.

That evening Roy and I were invited with other journalists and the entire Moscow diplomatic corps to a banquet in the Kremlin. On the way there Roy and I had discussed

the possibility of a fantastic scoop picture, and all we needed was permission to visit a Russian space station! After a sumptuous feast of suckling pigs, caviare and Russian champagne, beneath sparkling chandeliers in a setting straight out of *War and Peace*, Roy and I edged our way to within just a few yards of Khrushchev.

'Go on, Terry,' said Roy, shoving me closer. 'Ask him!'

'He'll never agree,' I whispered nervously. 'And we'll end up in bloody Siberia at this rate.'

Suddenly I found myself face to face with Khrushchev and his interpreter. Before I knew what I was saying I had blurted out our crazy proposition: 'Er . . . I . . . we . . . were wondering if it might be possible to visit your space centre. We'd like Mr Khrushchev's permission to take photographs there.' I made a camera-holding gesture.

The interpreter raised one eyebrow, then looked very grave for a moment before turning to Khrushchev and relaying our request to him.

Khrushchev listened intently, then turned towards me without expression, looking less and less like a friendly uncle. He stared into my eyes and I thought 'Christ! This is it', and waited for the worst. Then his old eyes twinkled, that big smile crossed his face and he started wagging his finger at me saying 'Niet! Niet!'

Roy and I hurried back to the Russian champagne.

Khrushchev was a larger-than-life character. He was above all, a great poser, and I always enjoyed photographing him. The last time I did so was on his tour of Scandinavia shortly before he was ousted from office. I had followed him on the tour but with little photographic success, until he appeared at a cattle show in some Swedish outpost. Suddenly he was surrounded by the beasts. Before the other photographers realized what I was doing, I scrambled across a fence and began to push my way through the cows towards him.

Khrushchev knew I wanted a picture and obligingly he grabbed a pair of reins that hung around the neck of a passing cow, and posed for me.

In the early sixties I, along with a great many others, looked upon John F. Kennedy with a kind of reverence. The clean, bright spirit of the Western World seemed to be embodied in the personality of this handsome young man; he was, quite simply, a living legend.

However, since those distant days many stories have emerged concerning his amorous exploits and so on and I've come to realize that he was no more, or less, than a normal human being, susceptible to normal human emotions and pressures.

I covered Kennedy's first visit to Europe. He arrived in Paris, with his wife, Jackie, and was welcomed by President de Gaulle with whom he posed for photographs at the Elysée Palace. Later that day Kennedy and de Gaulle drove through pouring rain along the Champs-Elysées to lay a wreath on the Tomb of the Unknown Soldier.

The tour moved on to Vienna where Kennedy met Khrushchev for talks on world peace. I photographed them together at the Opera as they sat on either side of the Austrian President, who seemed to symbolize for me the gulf which still exists between the two superpowers.

In June 1963 President Kennedy arrived in New Ross, Wexford, Eire to visit his Irish relatives at the Kennedy homestead where his grandfather had been born.

The imminent visit of the US President had caused a furore down on the farm and a thin layer of concrete had been hastily laid over the quagmire of cow-muck that normally formed the front yard. The President's security staff installed a hot line to the White House in the cow-shed so that he was ensured instant contact with Washington in case of a crisis.

In the farmyard stood several trestle tables laden with plates of sandwiches, home-made cakes and flans, all ready for the honoured guest to tuck into. The centre-

Khrushchev during his visit to London, 1956

Khrushchev and Kennedy, in Vienna, 1961. Between them is the President of Austria

piece of the splendid buffet was a cake iced with the crossed flags of Eire and the USA.

The lane leading to the farmyard was literally packed with locals, most of whom had been celebrating all morning in the local pub; the atmosphere was merry, to say the least. A few members of the local police, called in to hold back the crowd, had also been observed joining in the liquid celebrations, and they were having difficulty in performing their duty.

As the Presidential helicopter landed noisily behind the farmhouse, the locals hung onto their hats in the sudden breeze caused by the rotor blades. The herd of cows grazing in the nearby field, having previously ignored the elaborate proceedings, suddenly scattered in all directions.

Kennedy was given a tumultuous welcome by the crowd and as he stepped onto the farmyard concrete he was warmly embraced by his 64-year-old cousin, Mary Ryan. He kissed her cheek in return and then disappeared into the house for their family reunion.

A few minutes later, the Kennedy clan emerged to pose for photographs which we took in a few minutes. The President looked at the food on the tables, then a broad smile crossed his face, and he invited everyone to join in the feast.

The crowd cheered, the police in the barricade unlinked their arms and everyone surged forward onto the concrete which, being thin, immediately gave way under their combined weight. Cracks appeared everywhere, cow-muck oozed up between them and the smiling President appeared to be sinking.

The party was soon over after that and Kennedy had the cow-muck wiped from his shoes before climbing back aboard his helicopter which was soon airborne again. I never saw him again.

Prime Minister Harold Macmillan in Downing Street,
late fifties

Edith Sitwell, London, 1952

Mother Teresa at her 'Home for the Destitute and Dying',
Calcutta, 1969

145

Charlie Chaplin arrives back in London in 1952 after many years of living in the United States. On the roof of the Savoy Hotel with his wife Oona, he points out Kennington (the district where he was born)

Charlie Chaplin at the Savoy Hotel in 1966 after breaking his leg
Overleaf   Bing Crosby by river Thames at Chertsey, Surrey, 1961

Paul Robeson as Othello, Stratford-upon-Avon, 1959

Louis 'Satchmo' Armstrong, London, late 1950s

David Niven relaxes during the filming of *Candleshoe* in
which he played several parts

Peter Sellers as a London cabbie in the film *Prisoner of Zenda*

11

'Beautiful, just beautiful'

Beautiful women have been an essential ingredient in the staple diet of popular newspapers for at least as long as I've been in Fleet Street. In this category I include beautiful actresses publicizing their latest films or plays, fashion models showing off elegant creations and glamour girls displaying their ample charms.

For the photographer, this kind of work is very exacting and requires a certain measure of technical expertise – creating a beautiful image is a challenge which I welcome every now and again.

On a dull, rainy Sunday afternoon in 1951, Keystone sent me to photograph the departure of gorgeous Hollywood star Linda Darnell from the London Clinic where she had been recovering from a minor illness. At that time I had no flash-gun capable of synchronizing with my camera shutter, so I heaved along a large wooden tripod on which to steady my camera long enough for the exposure. The other photographers who turned up for the assignment with more sophisticated (and portable) equipment than my own stared at me in disbelief as I nervously set up my camera and tripod inside the foyer of the Clinic.

Miss Darnell appeared, wearing a fur coat, carrying a bouquet of flowers and looking even more beautiful than she did on the screen. My fellow photographers crowded around her: 'This way, Linda' . . . 'Can we have a smile, please' . . . 'Beautiful, just beautiful', they called out, as the famous lady posed for them. I was stuck at the back and felt completely lost.

Soon it was all over, the photographers began to pack up their cameras and Miss Darnell started to leave. She spotted me standing forlornly beside my hefty tripod.

'Did you want to take a picture, too?' she asked.

'Er . . . Yes, please. Could you sit there?' I asked, pointing to a nearby armchair.

Miss Darnell sat down and arranged herself in the chair. But in my nervousness I was all fingers and thumbs as I shifted the camera around to face her. To make matters worse my colleagues crowded around and began taking more pictures (my suggested pose must have been better than theirs!). Someone kicked my tripod and my cameras nearly fell to the floor.

The assignment was a total disaster for me. None of my pictures turned out and I

Jayne Mansfield arrives in London, 1957

thought back to the time I'd attempted to photograph Greta Garbo and Ivor Novello in the Temple Grounds long ago and it seemed that I might not be destined for this kind of work.

But over the years there were more lovely ladies to photograph and gradually I got the hang of things. Since then I've photographed many beauties. Often they have been in front of my lens for only the fraction of a second it takes to make a photograph. My subjects in the fifties and sixties included Jayne Mansfield, Marilyn Monroe, Vivien Leigh, Sophia Loren, Zsa Zsa Gabor, Judy Garland, Twiggy and many others.

It wasn't until I turned freelance that I took up glamour photography seriously. In 1971, newspapers started to publish pictures of
Vivien Leigh and Marilyn Monroe, London, 1956

topless girls – all very daring stuff – and I realized that I would have to broaden my horizons in that direction in order to compete with the Fleet Street glamour experts. I also realized that I would have to come up with something different, something extraordinary, in order to be successful in this particular field.

At the beginning of March 1971, I caught a morning rush-hour commuter train at Guildford bound for London where I was to attend a business meeting.

Looking out of the dirty, rain-streaked windows I saw the grey wintry weather lying like a wet blanket across the Surrey countryside. I was glad that I did not have to make this journey every day, as did most of my travelling companions. I was thankful that I'd chosen an unpredictable profession capable of whisking me off at a moment's notice to some exotic part of the world. I

Twiggy in the early 1960s

opened my morning newspaper, looking for possible picture-stories to follow-up. I smiled at the cartoons and turned the page, then something made me turn back again very quickly. Yes. There it was – depicted in the comic sketch – the perfect glamour assignment. Exactly what I had been looking for.

The cartoon was a variation on the old theme of a shipwrecked sailor marooned on a desert island with only a beautiful girl for companionship.

By the time the train pulled into Waterloo Station the story was almost complete in my mind's eye. I had recently visited the island of Abaco in the Bahamas and while there I'd been to a tiny uninhabited island five miles off the mainland. A friend had suggested that I should do a story about the place. Unfortunately, deserted islands do not in themselves mean very much to Fleet Street editors, so I had been unable to put forward the suggestion – until now. All I had to do was to find a beautiful woman, preferably

the most beautiful in London, willing to be 'shipwrecked' on the island with me, where I would photograph her as a beautiful cast-away.

By the time I got home I had developed the proposed situation a little further. It would be a genuine 'survival' story. The girl and I would survive for a week, living on our wits as real castaways would have to do, without food or water. Our only contact with civilization was to be a two-way radio link with the mainland, in case things went drastically wrong. After more consideration I decided to contact some friends of mine in the Special Air Service, to ask if they would give the lady in question a crash-course in survival – at which they were the undoubted experts. They agreed readily.

Next, I telexed my contact in the Bahamas asking him to set things up. Finally, when I knew that the whole idea was feasible, I contacted the *Sunday Mirror* and explained the idea to them. They were interested, and Roy Foster, the then Art Editor, agreed to come along as our anchor-man on Abaco.

So, all that remained was to find my beautiful companion. It was June who suggested that I invite Norwegian actress Julie Ege to join me. Julie lived in a luxury flat in Knightsbridge and the contrast between her sumptuous existence and the life of a castaway would add another interesting angle to the story.

Roy Foster and I took Julie out to lunch and outlined the idea to her. She was full of enthusiasm and agreed at once, although she was naturally saddened by the thought of having to leave her baby daughter, Joanna, behind in London for a week.

Julie took the SAS course; learning how to live without any of the aids of civilization – except for a survival knife, a magnifying glass, some plastic sheeting and a fishing-line. Among the few 'luxuries' we allowed ourselves were two hammocks made from parachute silk, and a container of fresh water for Julie's complexion.

Within a week we were on board a tiny boat taking us from Abaco to the tiny, unnamed island – we christened it 'No Name

Julie Ege 'Castaway' on 'No Name Cay', Bahamas, 1971

Cay'. As we waded ashore through the blue Caribbean I realized that the eternal cartoonist's fantasy had come true!

'No Name Cay' is no more than a mile long by half a mile wide – a strip of dazzling white coral sand dotted with palm trees, pines and, as we discovered to our cost, a particular kind of poison-ivy. The odd pieces of flotsam glinted in the sunlight on the beach; on closer inspection these turned out to be tin-cans and bottles; reminders of civilization across the water.

Our first duty was to light a driftwood fire using the magnifying glass to concentrate the sun's rays onto a pile of dried leaves. We made a water-trap, as instructed by the SAS, by stretching a sheet of plastic over a hole in the sand. At the bottom of the hole we placed a tin-can, in which to catch the drips of condensed water-vapour that collected on the underside of the sheet.

With these chores completed, Julie – one of the least inhibited ladies I know – took off all her clothes and stretched out on the sand to sunbathe, and I began taking photographs.

Julie and I got along famously as the week went by. Not a cross word passed between us although we managed to catch only one fish which we cooked on our fire. We also ate palm hearts and coconuts, drinking their milk from the shells.

The resulting pictures were marvellous and the series ran for four weeks in the *Sunday Mirror*.

When Julie and I returned to England, my friends made a great many jokes about my voluntary 'shipwreck'. No one could believe that we had not become lovers on the island.

Our situation was perhaps best illustrated by an incident which happened one morning on the island. I wanted to take a picture in which Julie would be clad in nothing more than a sheen of glistening sun-tan lotion. I began to apply the lotion to her back and legs, then I arrived at her breasts.

'You'd better do this bit yourself, Julie,' I said, a little embarrassed.

'Oh no, darling,' she replied. 'I don't want

to get lotion on my hands. I still have to do my hair. You just carry on.'

Picture the scene. Me. On a deserted island in the middle of nowhere, smoothing sun-tan lotion onto the most beautiful pair of breasts in the world. And I was pretending not to notice!

Julie is still a great friend of mine. I visited her recently at her home in Norway to produce a feature on her life today, and was pleased to learn that she has settled very happily in her own country.

The changing face of Lynn Frederick, taken during the course of ten years

12

All in a Day's Work

Just before Christmas 1964, I covered a train crash just outside Euston Station. A shunting engine had smashed into the cab of a 14-coach diesel train as it had pulled slowly out of the station. The cab of the diesel was crushed. Inside, trapped by the buckled metal, were the driver Cliff Alibone and his mate David Lindsay.

Lindsay, who was pinned in the cab by his seat, smoked cigarettes and drank mugs of tea while rescuers worked to free him. After 90 minutes they succeeded and before being taken to University College Hospital Lindsay asked how Alibone was doing.

The driver was in a much worse condition. It was almost impossible for the rescuers to use acetylene burners on the metal without causing him further agony. Slowly but surely the firemen worked, with crowbars, hacksaws and their bare hands, to make a narrow passage through the tangled wreckage, so that a doctor could adminster pain-killing injections and attach the blood-transfusion unit he had hung above the cab.

Finally, a massive railway crane was brought in to ease the other engine off the cab of the diesel, then winches were used to tear open the front of the cab. For one awful moment it seemed that the roof would fall in

on Alibone, but the winch-cables tautened and took the extra strain. Minutes later the pale-faced driver was visible, but still trapped by a four-inch-thick seat-stanchion. Thirty-seven hacksaw blades were worn out on the stanchion before he could finally be lifted from the cab.

Tragically, Cliff Alibone died in the operating theatre afterwards.

The famous shipbuilders Saunders-Roe had spent six years working on a secret project at their base in Cowes, Isle of Wight. Several intrepid cameramen had tried unsuccessfully to snatch a picture of the new craft in production. Approaches had been made from land, sea and air but each time the 'saucer', as it was known, was brought out into the open, security men stood by with huge camouflage nets ready to cover it again at the slightest suspicion of a photographer's presence.

I was not to be beaten, however, and together with my old friend Stanley Megaher I chartered a small aircraft and waited at Sandown airfield for a word from our reporter in Cowes that the 'saucer's' engines had started up. Taking off immediately we had

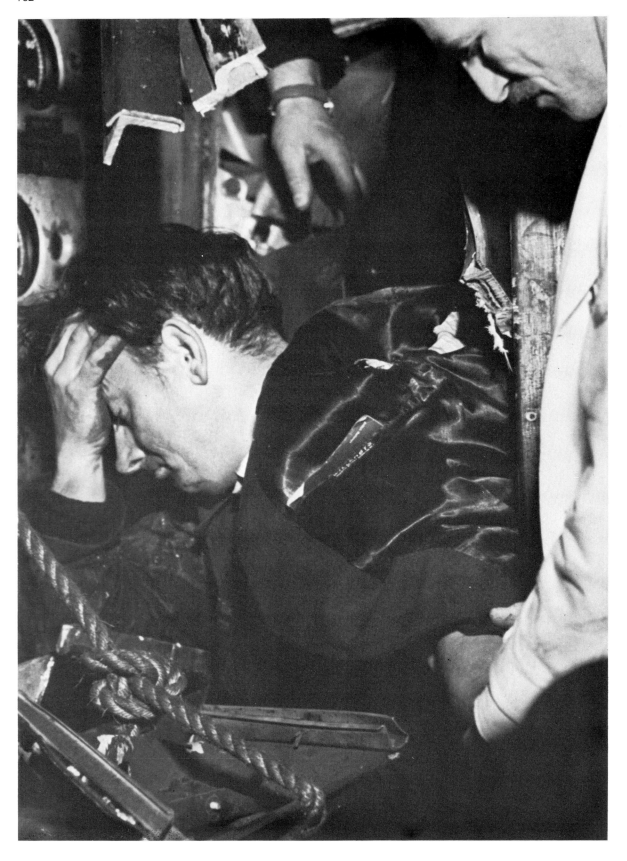

163

the go-ahead we were soon over Cowes and, as we approached the Saunders-Roe yard we told the pilot to throttle back and reduce the engine noise so that we could glide in undetected.

The whole operation was a success and the results were the first ever published pictures of a Hovercraft.

The biggest earthquake in Moroccan history occurred at the luxurious seaside resort of Agadir on 29 February 1960. The violent tremor lasted for just ten seconds, but the town collapsed like a fragile house of cards. Moments later a huge tidal wave added its force to the devastation. Agadir was plunged into darkness and all contact with the outside world was lost. Twenty thousand people died that night.

Next day, along with other correspondents, I was on board an old Dakota out of Blackbushe Airport, in Hampshire,

heading for Agadir, via Marseilles and Madrid. In Madrid we learned that planes were not being allowed to land in Agadir unless they were bringing in medical supplies. Although it was nearly midnight we managed to buy some supplies, thereby making our flight a legitimate one.

We landed a few miles outside Agadir at 3.00 a.m. It was too dark then for us to move into the town, but we could smell the burning buildings and could see the headlight beams of cars and lorries raking across the landscape every now and then, illuminating the scenes of devastation.

I managed to get transport into the town just before daybreak, with Freddie Reed of the *Daily Mirror*, Bill McConville of BCINA, Bill Beck of the *News Chronicle* and a BBC-TV film cameraman. Like most disasters that happen at night the real impact of the tragedy lay hidden in the darkness and, when daylight came, we were all shocked by the extent of the disaster.

Train crash at Euston Station, 1964

Agadir earthquake, 1960

Almost every building in the city had been flattened, as floor after floor had collapsed on top of each other so that holiday hotels now looked like enormous grotesque sandwiches.

Freddie Reed and I were wandering around the rubble together when a very distressed Englishman, wearing a pair of striped pyjamas, ran up to us crying 'My wife! My wife!' He told us they had been on holiday. He'd been in bed reading and his wife was in the bathroom when the earthquake struck. That was the last he had seen of her. The hotel collapsed and total darkness had engulfed him. The man had been trapped in bed, unable to move his legs. As time passed he had kept himself alive by drinking water from a vase of flowers, miraculously unbroken, on his bedside table. He was rescued but his wife was never found. There was little we could do for the man except give him some money and put him in touch with the British authorities.

I saw another man trapped with his wife beneath some iron girders. They had lain there, keeping each other's spirits up all night long, then the wife had died. Rescuers had to cut through her body to release the husband although his arm had to be amputated before he could be pulled free.

We stayed in Agadir for two more days, based at the airport and sleeping on the floor of a large hangar with survivors who were waiting to be flown out to hospitals in nearby countries. The daytime heat, mixed with the smell of decaying bodies, was unbearable and we soaked handkerchiefs with *eau de cologne* and tied them over our mouths and noses to get some relief from the stench. Rats were seen running among the rubble and naturally the authorities feared a major health hazard. Vast graves were dug by bulldozers in which unidentified bodies were buried in quicklime.

I was glad when the Dakota flew in to pick us up and take us home, via Casablanca where we were to spend the night. Before we were allowed back on board a medical orderly sprayed our clothing with DDT

Agadir earthquake, 1960

powder.

It was late evening when we eventually booked into an elegant hotel in Casablanca, tired, dirty and unshaven. We sat at the bar discussing the earthquake. I ordered some food but was told by the barman that the restaurant was closed for the night. I was about to vent my anger at the barman when a very beautiful woman who had overheard our conversation stepped up to the bar and offered to take us to a restaurant nearby. My companions declined the offer saying they were too tired to leave the hotel. I went with the lady to what turned out to be one of Casablanca's top restaurants. Diners at nearby tables looked askance at me, looking and smelling as I did like a tramp.

Next day, our flight to London was delayed by five hours, and, like a fool, I drank a few glasses of red wine then lay out in the sun beside the departure lounge. I slept for two hours then awoke with terrible sunstroke. I was sick on the way home. When I got there I stripped off all my clothes inside the front door, having been advised to destroy them by the health officials in Agadir. June took them into the garden and burnt the lot.

Another set of my clothes had to be burned in the garden when, in the winter of 1961, I returned from covering a smallpox epidemic in Karachi, Pakistan. *Daily Herald* reporter Brian Woosey and I had managed to get into one of the city's smallpox isolation hospitals, by inviting a health official to our hotel and sharing a bottle of Scotch with him. At first he had been reluctant to take us to the hospital but as the level of the bottle gradually went down he changed his mind and insisted on driving us there himself.

The official waved aside an armed guard at the main gate, and within minutes we found ourselves inside an emergency smallpox ward, which was no more than a ramshackle tin-roofed shed containing wooden beds held together with rope. Sunlight poured in through the open side of the ward emphasizing the smoke and dust drifting everywhere. A group of people stood

A hospital during smallpox epidemic, Karachi, 1961

around the bed of a youth who was just a few minutes away from death. A closer look at some of the victims revealed pock-marked faces, running sores and peeling skin. Luckily our senses were somewhat dulled by the whisky we'd drunk earlier, otherwise I don't think we could have stood being there for long. At one point I placed a plank of wood across an open dustbin on which to stand to get a better angle. Unfortunately I slipped and my camera-bag dropped into the bin half-filled with used and yellowing swabs! I pulled it out again as quickly as possible.

On returning to London we drove straight from the airport to the *Daily Herald* office where Foreign Editor John Graham ordered us away from his desk until we'd been cleared by a doctor. Back home I bathed again in disinfectant and with my clothes sending smoke into the South London sky I began to feel clean again. But, two days later, I began to develop a sore throat. I went to my local GP and told him about my recent visit to Karachi. He told me not to worry and sent me home with tablets for my throat. Next morning the doctor knocked at my front door having had second thoughts. He then proceeded to inoculate the entire family, including my mother-in-law who was staying with us. 'Ooh, my Gawd!' she exclaimed in her cockney accent, 'and I've never been further than Southend!'

The Profumo Affair hit the headlines in the summer of 1963, and during the following months every British newspaper devoted many column-inches to the scandal that shook Westminster.

Mandy Rice-Davies was a pretty, young girl whose name, along with that of Christine Keeler and others, was closely connected with the story. As a result, anything to do with Mandy became very big news indeed. One day the *Daily Express* were given an exclusive tip-off that she was having a holiday in Majorca. Consequently I was assigned to join a reporter on the island where I was to take some glamorous shots of Mandy while at the same time ensuring that no other newspaperman got anywhere within picture-taking distance of her.

The reporter introduced me to Mandy in her hotel room. She was indeed an attractive girl and I was greatly impressed with her especially as she was in the act of pulling a stocking up a very attractive leg at the time.

The assignment was relatively easy as there was little work involved once I had taken my pictures. One morning Mandy invited me on a walk along the beach. I locked my camera in my hotel room and joined her immediately, ready to keep my eyes peeled for reporters. Mandy's great beauty attracted much attention on the beach and proved too much for one lecherous Spaniard who brazenly walked up and pinched her bottom. Mandy swung around and clobbered the unfortunate man with her handbag. His face distorted with pain and surprise, and the contents of the handbag – make-up, mirror, purse, etc – went flying in all directions. I watched what happened as though looking at a slow-motion film sequence and I thought 'What a great picture!' And I, for once, was camera-less.

Mandy definitely stood out in a crowd. A little farther along the beach she was spotted by a Fleet Street reporter holidaying with his wife. I saw what I'd thought was my exclu-

Mandy Rice-Davies, Majorca, 1963

DAILY EXPRESS THURSDAY AUGUST 15 1963

PHOTO NEWS

The only man who knows

Lord Denning, inquiry almost ended, sits behind wall of files labelled 'Top Secret'

PICTURE BY TERRY FINCHER

'The only man who knows', Lord Denning, *Daily Express,* 15 August 1963

sive story dissolving before my very eyes as he bounded up to me.

'Hello, Terry,' he said while slapping me on the back. 'Who's the bird?'

'It's a . . . er . . . girl-friend,' I said.

He winked at me knowingly as if to say 'Your secret's safe with me.' I was astonished that he actually believed me, and thankful that he had obviously never seen a picture of Mandy. I declined his offer to join him and his wife for a drink and hurriedly steered Mandy back towards our hotel.

During the Profumo Affair I, like most of my Fleet Street rivals, spent a great deal of time waiting outside the Home Office to photograph the arrivals and departures of people attending the official inquiry into the security services. The inquiry was being conducted inside the building by Lord Denning.

For me it was a dull, routine assignment, and after a few days of frustration I decided to aim for something better. Together with a colleague I went around to the back door of

the Home Office. I scribbled a note to Lord Denning asking if I might photograph him at work. I then handed the note to a commissionaire with a half-crown tip. Much to my surprise a reply came ten minutes later. His Lordship *agreed* to our request!

A Home Office official led us to the second floor office where Lord Denning greeted us warmly. He was a charming man and I believe he was glad of a break. He was seated behind a large desk which was literally covered in paperwork. A row of 'Top Secret' files formed a line along the front of his desk. As I photographed him behind this 'wall of work' he wearily told me that the files contained approximately 850,000 words, I took a few exposures then we took our leave.

Out in the street the opposition watched us walk away.

'Giving up so soon?' someone called out.

Rooftop drama, London, mid 1960s. The man was threatening to throw himself and his child off the roof. The situation was saved by the prompt action of the policewoman edging closer

The homeless people who sleep in the streets of Bombay, 1964

A shepherd in Bethlehem, Christmas 1969

Hungarian refugee at a camp in Linz, Austria, 1958

Overleaf
'The Green March', Spanish Sahara, Morocco, 1975

In 1970 I flew to Beirut, Lebanon, hoping to photograph Leila Khaled, the PFLP member who had been involved in the hijacking of an El Al plane. The plane had eventually landed at Heathrow in London, one of her comrades was killed in the attempt and Leila herself had been arrested by the British police and later deported to Lebanon.

On arrival in Beirut I went to the PFLP offices to request an interview with her. Security men with bulging jackets lounged on the stairs outside the office door, and one of them took me inside to meet their spokesman, Ghassan Kanafani, who told me I would have to be patient and wait at my hotel for a decision.

I booked in as usual at the Palm Beach Hotel where I lounged around the swimming-pool for the following two weeks, every so often visiting the PFLP offices, in an attempt to get my pictures. On one occasion I was having a conversation with Kanafani and he proceeded to tell me more about myself than I already knew. It was an example of the efficiency of their intelligence network and I was very impressed.

One evening, feeling utterly bored, I went out for a few drinks with an old friend. I had my fair share of whisky in his company and eventually back at the hotel I retired at 3.30 a.m.

The telephone rang at 6.15 a.m. I awoke to its sound with a terrible hangover. The receptionist told me that a lady was waiting to see me downstairs. I staggered into my clothes and – via the bathroom, where I was violently sick – made my way to the lobby.

Leila Khaled, accompanied by two obviously armed bodyguards, was waiting for me. She looked very attractive in a pink jumper and dark trousers. The introductions over, I went back to my room to collect my cameras – and to be sick again.

It was a warm and pleasant morning but it did little to improve my delicate state of health as we rode in a Cadillac along the wide boulevards. I asked if we might stop at a garage, so I could use the toilet.

Back in the car Leila said, 'You had too much to drink last night, didn't you? If you were a Muslim you wouldn't have a hangover.'

We drove on to a Palestinian refugee camp where I saw the terrible conditions they had to live in. I photographed Leila with her grandfather. She also posed for me with some Russian-made weapons. I was given some coffee and began to feel better as we talked, with her bodyguards looking on. Leila spoke of her arrest in London. She told me that the British police had been very nice to her and that when she eventually left the police station they'd given her a wig to disguise her from the Press. She was an intelligent and charming young woman and I found it difficult to believe that she was capable of a hijack.

Leila Khaled has remained faithful to the Palestinian cause and is now married. Kanafani was assassinated by the Israelis in 1972.

My mother was always proud of her homeland and a couple of times during my early teens she took me across the sea to Ireland on board the Liverpool–Belfast ferry to visit her family and friends.

I've always found the Irish people to be warm and friendly and more than generous with their hospitality. But, even as a young man, I sensed the tension that existed in Northern Ireland. Later, of course, I was to experience the 'Troubles' at first-hand.

In the late sixties violence erupted in the Province and an awareness of the 'Irish Problem' grew once more in the public conscience. British troops were called in following sectarian riots in Belfast and Londonderry. Since then the world's Press has flocked to Northern Ireland to cover the country which has been torn apart by bloody conflict.

For me Belfast city centre is symbolic of the 'Troubles', an example being the all-too-familiar barricades where one has to be searched before entering the main shopping area.

Leila Khaled, Palestinian Refugee Camp, Beirut, 1970
Overleaf
The Bogside, Londonderry, Northern Ireland

Northern Ireland is always a depressing assignment, and it was never more so than on the occasion of the funeral of the Maguire children in August 1976. One afternoon in the Andersontown area of Belfast Mrs Maguire had been taking her three children (one a baby in a pram) for a walk in the sunshine. As she pushed the pram along the pavement British soldiers were pursuing an IRA getaway car when a sudden burst of gunfire sent it careering wildly onto the pavement towards the mother and her children. Mrs Maguire was critically injured: and her children were crushed to death. One IRA man also died in the crash.

Following the tragedy two women, Betty Williams and Mairead Corrigan, sister of Mrs Maguire, launched an appeal among the women of Northern Ireland to support a massive demonstration against the violence which surrounded their lives. Up to that time some 1,500 lives had been lost in the troubles since 1969. Yet it had taken the deaths of these innocents to give birth to the Peace People Movement.

Betty Williams (left) and Mairead Corrigan, founders of the Peace People Movement in Northern Ireland

Guildford pub bombing, 1974

Shortly after the funeral I got to know Betty and Mairead and on one occasion travelled with them from Belfast to Birmingham to attend a peace rally.

On the evening of Saturday 5 October 1974, I was relaxing at home when I received a 'phone call from a magazine informing me that a bomb had exploded in a pub in nearby Guildford. I was there within minutes.

The scenes outside the Horse and Groom, a pub frequented by young soldiers from nearby army camps, were chaotic as policemen, firemen and ambulancemen dealt with the casualties. The bomb had been left in a crowded alcove and seven people had been killed in the explosion.

I had taken a few pictures when there was a second explosion in the Seven Stars, another pub only a few hundred yards down the street. I ran along the street in time to see the landlord being brought out, his head bleeding badly. Immediately my thoughts went back to London during the blitz, and I

coupled those memories with the violence now happening in my home town. I hoped that this would be the last time the people of this charming old English market-town would see such violence.

Fortunately some news assignments are more light-hearted, such as the time in the mid sixties when almost every newspaper carried the story of Chi-Chi and An-An, the two giant pandas upon whose successful reproduction depended the future of their species. Unfortunately, despite several attempts to mate them, Chi-Chi and An-An hadn't yet got it together. Someone (I can't exactly recall who, but I think he worked on the *Daily Express* picture-desk) came up with what seemed a brilliant idea for a picture feature on the love-struck animals. Basically it was this: I would take a photograph of Chi-Chi in her cage at London Zoo, have a giant enlargement made, take it to Moscow, put it inside An-An's cage and photo-

graph him gazing longingly at his girl-friend's image. Simple. The enlargement was duly made. It measured 7 x 4 ft and was mounted on hardboard. My first problem came at London Airport when airline officials insisted that I put the picture in the baggage-hold of the plane. However, they couldn't guarantee that the picture wouldn't get damaged and I was eventually allowed to lay it across the two seats beside me.

In Moscow the Russian Customs and Immigration officials eyed me as though I was a lunatic, and by the time my translated explanation reached their ears I'm sure they were fully convinced of my insanity. We all ended up having a good laugh together; but I've a strong suspicion that they were merely humouring me, though they did find me some string with which to tie the enlargement on top of the taxi which was to take me to my hotel in Red Square.

My old friend, AP photographer Brian Calvert, was based in Moscow at the time and he came to see me at the hotel where he

In-flight shot of Chi-Chi en route to Moscow to meet An-An, mid 1960s

bought me a much-needed drink. He asked me why I was carting a bloody great picture of a panda around Moscow, and I explained the brilliant idea to him.

'You'll have a job getting into the zoo, mate,' he said. 'There's been an outbreak of foot and mouth disease and the zoo is in quarantine.'

Naturally this news came as quite a blow, but I was determined not to go home without a picture of An-An gazing at Chi-Chi's photograph. After a few more drinks I enlisted the help of a young newsfilm cameraman and together we took the blow-up to the zoo where we walked around the perimeter fence until we found a gate that swung open. We went in.

Straw lay everywhere, the place reeked of disinfectant and the only sounds came from within the cages. We were tip-toeing towards the panda pen when two guards grabbed us and demanded to see our papers. With the language difficulties as well it was impossible for us to explain exactly what we were doing in their closed zoo with an enormous picture of a panda!

I never got the shot I wanted and eventually I presented the enlargement to the *Daily Express* office in Moscow, where it graced the wall for many years.

Shortly after this incident I flew back to Moscow with the real thing. Chi-Chi was being transported to Russia for the attempt to mate her with An-An. She was given Very Important Panda treatment by BEA. They had replaced the usual Comet with a larger aircraft and even removed several seats so that her cage would fit into the first-class compartment. Unfortunately the whole venture proved to be a bit of a flop for the two pandas still didn't fancy one another.

During a visit to Cyprus in the sixties I was invited with several other journalists to a party in the sergeants' mess of the Parachute Regiment. It was a boozy occasion and at one point in the proceedings someone among the Press corps challenged the Paras to a race for possession of the piano. A tre-

mendous rough and tumble followed, resulting in a victory for the Press. As we all piled on the piano one of the Paras issued a challenge in return. He claimed that there was no journalist capable of doing the Paras' job, so why didn't one of us learn how to parachute? He argued that, surely, in a combat situation, such a skill would be more than useful to a correspondent. Before I knew it I, in my usual enthusiastic way, had accepted the challenge. I put up the idea to the *Daily Express* and they agreed.

A year later, now in 10 Para Territorials, I had to pass a gruelling physical aptitude test before I could go on to final training at Abingdon. I found this training particularly heavy going as I was by then in my mid-thirties and nowhere near as agile as the 18-20-year-old lads who were also on the course. At the end of each day's training I would lie on my bed totally exhausted, with every muscle aching and the echoes of the instructor's voice still ringing in my ear,

Making a parachute jump over Oxfordshire, 1965 (the camera was strapped to my boot)

'Red on . . . Green on . . . Go!' However, I persevered and after two weeks I'd completed eight jumps and gained my 'wings'.

Although I've never 'dropped' on a military operation, my parachuting experience came in handy on several stories even if the assignments themselves weren't particularly successful. On one occasion three army padres were due to be 'dropped' on Hankley Common, in Surrey. The exercise had all the ingredients of a good picture-story, and the *Daily Express* wanted me to jump with the padres to photograph them on the way down.

However, on the big day the wind velocity was very close to the allowed limit and we were told that although we would take off there was little chance that we'd actually make the jump.

Our Hercules was soon approaching the dropping zone and that's when the officer-in-charge told us we would be jumping, after all – wind velocity or no. The army had done something of a PR job for the event, inviting photographers, reporters and TV news-crews, all waiting on the Common, and I believe we were committed to putting on a show. A prominent Bishop was on board and he blessed us before we jumped. 'Very nice,' I thought. 'It's good to have the Lord on your side when you're doing this kind of work!'

'RED ON– GREEN ON – GO!' came the order. I was the last in the 'stick' out of the door. Once my 'chute opened I looked around for the padres. I saw them, drifting in the opposite direction, taken by the wind away from the landing-zone, and I decided that it was hardly worth taking out my camera. Looking down I saw the cluster of newsmen waiting to greet us, their faces looking up towards me. I landed stylishly in front of a TV newsreel camera, at the same time noticing that the three padres had landed more than a hundred yards away. I released my 'chute and pulled off my helmet, then I heard the disappointed cameraman exclaim: 'Christ! It's bloody Fincher!'

13

'A drink for your thoughts, Terry?'

Among my favourite assignments was a fantastic walk I took in the Himalayas in 1969, in search of the legendary Gurkhas, the brave little warriors who had fought alongside the British Army in Malaya, North Africa, Burma and in other campaigns, and were now returned to their mountain villages. In fact, some of these old soldiers were Victoria Cross holders, due to receive back-dated pensions awarded by the British government.

While making arrangements for this journey, a young Gurkha officer – proud of the fact that he had recently completed the Sandhurst officers' course – was assigned to accompany me as a guide and to deliver one of the pensions personally. Also with us, to carry our equipment, were two Sherpa porters.

Our departure point was the British Gurkha camp at Paklihawa, Nepal, not far from the Indian border. Just before setting out we heard that one of them, a VC holder, was already on his way into the camp to collect his pension. So we went out to meet him as he came across the paddy-fields. He greeted us with a broad grin and a smart salute. He was dressed in a suit which had seen better days, but which in true Gurkha

tradition was still kept smart. He told me it had been bought for him at Burtons when he came to London to receive his Victoria Cross from the Queen many years earlier. He explained that he badly needed his pension to save his farm up in the hills. Despite his 47 years he looked fit and young in comparison with some of his fellow countrymen (life expectancy in that region of the Himalayas at that time was cruelly short).

After saying farewell to the old soldier we made our way by Land Rover to the town of Tansing, some 6,000 ft up in the foothills, where the air began to get noticeably fresher. The road stopped at Tansing and from then on for us it was to be hard foot-slogging, all the way.

We began walking in a zig-zagging semi-circle towards Pokhara. I felt sorry for the two Sherpas carrying our gear in baskets on their backs, but they didn't seem to mind as they were used to such work. Indeed, the weight they were supporting seemed next to nothing compared to the loads belonging to other travellers we passed along the route. Men, women and children carry everything in the hills – by tradition they won't use donkeys or mules.

The first few miles out of Tansing were

184

reasonably easy and in the far distance I could see the snow-capped Himalayan peaks. But they were soon lost to sight as we dropped down into thick jungle valleys and passed many hamlets and farms. The rice in the paddy-fields had turned golden and was ready for the harvest. Brightly coloured parrots swooped down to raid the crop and I saw irate farmers chasing monkeys out of the fields.

Word of our journey arrived at villages before we did. The news was out that a white man was coming. Whenever I entered a village, people approached me, asking for medical attention as though I was some sort of saviour. One man brought to me had a broken, gangrenous leg. All I could do was to advise his family to get him to the nearest medical aid centre, which was several days' walk away.

The Sherpas spent as many nights as they could in huts in the villages along the route, drinking the potent local wine and enjoying the hospitality of the villagers while exchanging gossip picked up along the way. It was clear that this was the way that news travelled throughout the region. I had no desire to sleep in the huts as they were usually full of smoke and mosquitoes and each night before leaving me the Sherpas would

Sgt Nabahadur Thapa salutes, with his wife in the background

pitch my tent near the village.

In each village as the sun sank behind the mountains the local children would creep up to my tent and after some persuasion I would often get them singing to the music of my portable tape-recorder.

One night, when the children had gone and the wind was whistling around my tent, I heard a shuffling followed by a sniffing sound. Then a wild dog stuck its head through the tent-flap and began growling at me. I became aware of the presence of other dogs outside and realized I was surrounded by a pack. I picked up the long stick I'd been using to walk with, and clouted the animal across the snout with it. The wild dog yelped and backed out of the tent. But the animals hung around for hours and I lay awake all night waiting for them to leave.

The journey went on, across rickety suspension-bridges and through narrow passes. One stretch was down the steep side of a mountain which seemed to me like a sheer drop into oblivion!

The Gurkha officer found his VC winner, Sgt Nabahadur Thapa, in the village of Litung. He was a small, wizened old man of eighty, with one eye – the other had been cut out by the local medicine man a year or so before. Scattering chickens in all directions, the old man laid a straw mat out for us in his hut. All around him, playing in the dust, were several children who, I noticed, were prone to answering the call of nature whenever or wherever the moment arose. Several small pigs and a few dogs turned up as we sat talking to the old man in the gathering gloom of evening.

Early next morning Nabahadur Thapa, (dressed in ill-fitting denims with his Gurkha cap set at a jaunty angle on his head and his medals pinned on with an old safety-pin) walked with his wife, who wore large gold ear-rings and a ring through her nose, to a seat beneath the pipal trees, where I photographed them.

There were other old soldiers in other villages and one place had no less than 18 local farmers who had served with the British at one time or another. In another an old Gurkha VC had recently died of tuber-culosis. His wife would not meet us as she had never been photographed before and had become a recluse since the death of her husband. But I was taken to the maize field which the man had tended since his retirement from the army; and there, mounted on a stick for all to see, were his medals.

We reached a point within 20 miles of Annapurna and Dhaulagiri, which we could see towering in the distance, before turning towards Pokhara. On the way we passed several porters loaded with army kit belonging to Gurkhas made redundant by government defence cuts.

The trek among the Gurkha villages took two weeks. I walked over 120 miles and lost almost a stone in weight. The only signs of civilization I saw in all that time were a commercial aircraft which had flown over at the beginning of the walk, a few Seiko watches and some transistor radios brought back by the soldiers returning to the hills.

As I crossed the last stretch of plain before Pokhara I saw my first white person in two weeks, an attractive-looking woman riding towards me on a horse.

'Good morning,' I said to her as she rode by.

She passed without a word or acknowledgement of any kind, and I knew then that I was back in civilization.

It was 1979 and, sitting alone with my thoughts on the veranda of the Norfolk Hotel in Nairobi, I watched another African day slip into night. I had been in Kenya for a few days chasing American rock singer Linda Ronstadt and Governor Jerry Brown of California. Now the assignment was over, the Governor and the singer had gone back to America, and I was beginning to relax a little.

My reverie was interrupted by an American journalist, an old friend, who sat down beside me.

'A drink for your thoughts, Terry?' he offered.

He bought me another Sundowner and, still in a pensive mood, I proceeded to tell him my thoughts about Africa, the Dark

Continent, and the way it has changed even in my lifetime. I had been many times to Nairobi en route to some assignment or another. I had often listened to tales about the old farmers in the bush and about the white hunters who had set out on safari from this very spot, and I knew that the roar of the lions could once be heard here by hotel guests. It seemed a sad thing that those days were gone and, with them, some of the great characters too.

'You know, you're wrong about that,' said the American. 'You should meet Tony Fitzjohn and George Adamson. They are what Africa, the bush and wildlife are all about today.'

He told me of the Adamson/Fitzjohn project to rehabilitate lions that had been either born or held in captivity and return them to the wild, at Kora Game Reserve, on the Tana River.

Of course I knew of George Adamson and his wife, Joy, of *Born Free* fame, but I had no idea who this Tony Fitzjohn was. It so happened that Tony was, at the time, on one of his rare visits to Nairobi, and my friend offered to introduce me to him.

Tony Fitzjohn turned out to be a tall, athletic man in his late twenties with a restlessness about him that reminded me of a caged animal. I liked him immediately although at first I found it difficult to get through to him; he seemed too easily distracted by the chatter of the tourists or the pretty girls passing by. But gradually, throughout the evening I learned the Tony Fitzjohn story.

He was an orphan from London who had been adopted at the age of three by a bank clerk and his wife. He attended good schools in England, but in his teens his adventurous spirit manifested itself when he left a cosy job in an English dairy company and set out for South Africa. After many adventures there, and nurturing a fast-growing love for African wildlife, he arrived in Mombasa, Kenya, still searching for his place in life.

George Adamson, Tony Fitzjohn and friends, 1979

Overleaf
Tony Fitzjohn *('Mtoto simba')* runs across Kora landscape, 1979

That's when he heard about the possibility of a job with George Adamson at Kora. Adamson's previous assistant had been killed by a lion and Tony managed to persuade George that *he* was the right man to replace him. Tony soon earned himself the Swahili nickname *Mtoto simba* – 'Lion boy'.

I told Tony that I would like very much to visit him and George at Kora – and he promised to think about it and keep in touch.

Six weeks later the arrangements had been made and I flew from London to Nairobi, looking forward to recording what I knew to be one of the last great African adventures. Tony met me in his Land Rover and before leaving Nairobi I stocked it up with food supplies and crates of beer, a few bottles of gin and some orange juice, for such luxuries were in short supply in the bush.

On the way we stopped for the night in a small village. Tony knew the local priest there, a young Irishman who rode around on a large motorcycle, who invited us to a village party to be held that evening to celebrate a Kenyan national holiday. The village chief's wife, a very large woman, had a motherly affection for Tony, and locals, young and old alike, approached him wide-eyed and fascinated by the scars on his neck that he'd received during a lion attack. '*Mtoto simba*,' they whispered, reaching out to touch him as if he might not be real. Tony let out the occasional 'roar', for fun, which sent them scattering in fits of laughter.

Later, under the glow of a single electric-light bulb, we joined the chief and his wife in a kind of village hall packed with locals. They were swaying to and fro to music provided by two badly scratched records, belonging to the priest, which they played on a battery-operated record-player.

Next day we continued our journey to Kora camp which turned out to be little more than a few straw huts inside a small compound bordered by a wooden fence. A rickety gate stood open for us and George Adamson waited to greet us. He was dressed only in shorts and sandals and sported a short goatee beard and a veritable mane of long grey hair. His skin was tanned

dark and he looked a picture of good health.

Lunch was prepared by an African cook on an open wood fire and served up in one of the huts which was completely open at one side affording a splendid view of the bush-land beyond. The appearance of the food brought many other visitors scurrying from the bush, namely wild birds and squirrels. Overhead, on a pole supporting the roof, lay a large monitor lizard which occasionally flicked open its eyes to look down at us. Lunch was brought to an abrupt halt when a large guinea-fowl flapped clumsily in, knocking everything flying!

That afternoon Tony and I drove out into the bush, stopping every so often to look at animal tracks in the dirt. 'A snake crossed here' or 'Lion passed this way this morning,' he would say. He was aware of every sound in the landscape and seemed able to understand its meaning. 'I learned it all from George,' he said, in genuine admiration. 'He really is a marvellous old man.'

In the evening the three of us sat in silence beneath the vast African sky watching the sun go down beyond the trees, and cradling glasses of the gin and orange I'd brought from Nairobi. It was one of the most memorable experiences of my life, comparable to my Himalayan walk nine years earlier. The night sounds drifted in from the bush, but still no one spoke. Each of us was lost in his own thoughts.

The not-too-distant roar of a lion brought me sharply back to reality, and I felt a little uneasy for the compound fence looked none too sound.

Soon the oil lamp was lit and dinner was served. This time an entirely different collection of animals appeared on the table – several mice and other furry creatures. One remarkable animal even had his own tin of nuts which he was able to open all by himself.

George and Tony discussed the possible whereabouts of their own lions. They knew the nearby roar came from a stranger and they were a little concerned that their own beasts, recently released into the wild, were not yet capable of hunting their own food. It was decided to purchase a dead camel from

a Somali village market some distance away so that the Kora lions could eat.

Next morning I accompanied George on a drive far out into the bush. He stopped the battered Land Rover at one point and climbed onto its roof, carrying in his hand a box-like gadget connected to an aerial and earphones. He then scanned the countryside with the tracking equipment, hoping to pick up signals from those of his lions wearing radio-collars.

'They're growing up and moving away,' he said sadly.

Later, completely unarmed, we began to track down a lioness and her cubs. After a while we stopped walking and George called out a message in 'Lion Language' and to my amazement he received an answer from behind some rocks a short distance away. Eventually we got close enough to see the lioness and her cubs playing together. This was ample reward for George for it was a lioness he had released from Kora some time ago and he was pleased to see that she had mated successfully in the wild.

On the way back to camp we stopped to rest, and drink gin and orange from a flask, at a spot overlooking the Tana river. George talked at length of his great love for Africa and his lions. He recalled with fondness the 1930s, when he and others had tracked all the way up to Lake Rudolf, pitching their tents for the night within a fence made from thorn bushes to keep horses and men safe from the jackals and hyenas. These days he found himself more and more saddened by man's destruction of the land and his beloved wildlife.

I tried to draw him out on the subject of his wife, Joy, but he would say little about her except that he spoke to her from time to time on the camp radio. (Since then of course, Joy Adamson has died, having been murdered at her jungle camp in Kenya.)

I stayed with George and Tony for just over a week, savouring every moment of their primitive existence except, perhaps, for the stench of the decaying camel carcass (which lay not far from my cabin just outside the compound fence) and the presence, one evening, of the lions who came to feed on its remains. It was amazing to watch Tony actually 'talking' with the beasts – not in a roar that I had expected but a low, guttural, panting sound.

Another evening George and Tony pulled out a dust-covered box containing their collection of photographs, and some of George's dated back to the thirties and were yellow with age. It was a fascinating collection, an absolute mine of memories for George and a snapshot history of Kenya for me. Later that same evening Tony got me involved with developing some pictures in the darkroom inside his hut in which he used an enlarger powered by a 12-v car battery and water siphoned from an old oildrum filled from the Tana river. It was the first time in my photographic career that I'd experienced the prospect of photographs 'fogged' by moonlight. We made several prints and laid them on the solar dryer 'built by George' to dry in the sun next morning.

All I have left of that trip are my own photographs and my own memories – of the tiny encampment surrounded by wild animals, of the camp shower which was no more than a bucket with nail holes punched in its bottom, of the toilets made from the enormous skulls of dead elephants and of shaking out my shoes each morning to ensure there were no spiders or scorpions lurking inside them. On the last day Tony and I cleared a bumpy runway beside the camp and I was picked up by a small chartered plane and flown across the bushland to Nairobi.

I returned to Nairobi again a year later en route to yet another African assignment. But this one was in complete contrast to my stay at Kora – it was the most horrifying story of human suffering and misery I have ever covered.

My destination was the tiny village of Kaabong in the Karamoja district of Uganda where a devastating famine was at its height. Despite relief-aid schemes there were great difficulties in getting food into the area and many tens of thousands had died from hunger.

I travelled from Nairobi to Kaabong with Paul Dhillion, a TV cameraman who knew the area well. We drove for two days for 700 miles along a dusty, winding track in a battered saloon car which had over 100,000 miles on the clock. It was the only car which the hire company would allow on a trip into the Karamoja district. We stopped at Moroto to have punctures repaired and re-fuel the car and spare petrol-cans. On the way to Kaabong we were stopped every so often by young men dressed in semi-military uniforms and carrying automatic rifles, with bandoliers of ammunition slung across their shoulders: we never knew if they were soldiers or bandits. They were invariably nervous and anxious to know what we were carrying. Some of them even thought I was a priest.

'Have you food or water, Father?' they would ask.

We gave them what we could, which wasn't much for we needed the small amount of extra supplies for ourselves.

Going along with my new-found persona, I said 'Bless you, my son,' on one occasion to one angry young man. It seemed to do the trick for we were soon on our way again.

At first glance Kaabong looked an attractive place. The surrounding landscape suggested fertility with tall grass and wild flowers swaying in the breeze.

But as we approached the mission we saw the first of the walking skeletons – a young child with protruding ribs and legs barely covered with flesh. Then we saw more and more of those wretched and helpless children. One little skeleton sucked at its mother's withered breast. There were so many staring eyes and swollen bellies that it was hard to believe these were human beings.

We met Father Liapetti, the Italian priest who ran the mission. He showed us a queue of people, young and old, and waiting hopefully for food. Many of them had walked from outlying villages in the hope of finding food there. Some had died on the way.

Overleaf
Too weak to stand, a young girl lies dying on the ground, Kaabong, Karamoja, 1980

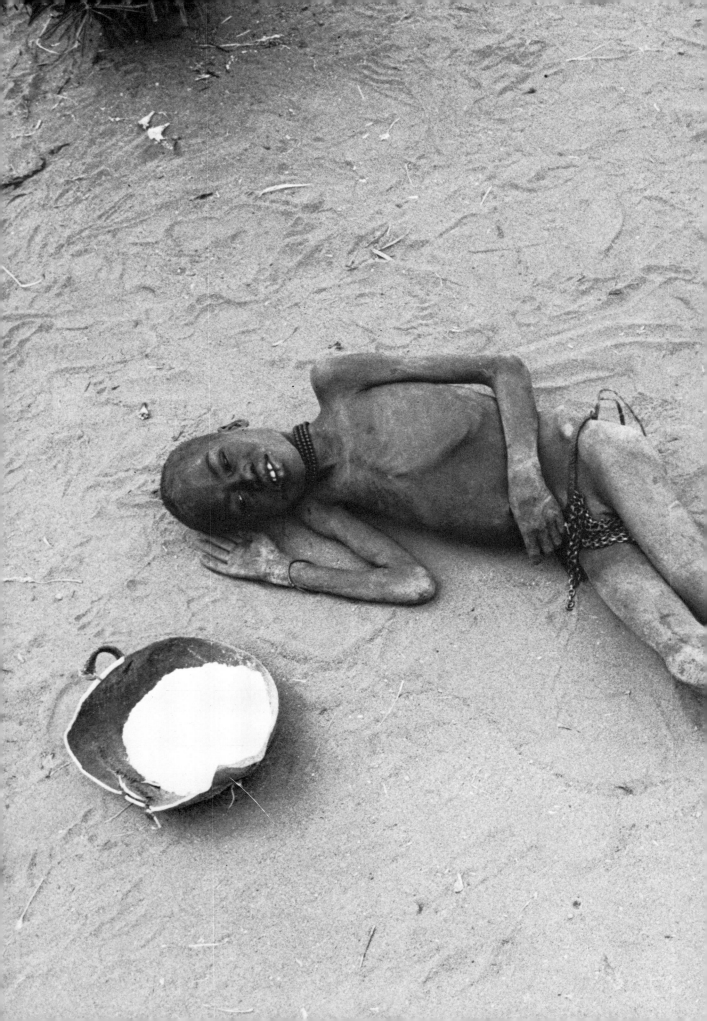

194

He took us to the village school where a
'Save the Children' feeding programme was
in operation, but even that seemed a hope-
less task when seen in its proper perspec-
tive. One little boy dropped dead in front of
my camera. Not far away another child had
curled up and died.

Early each morning Father Liapetti held a
mass funeral for those who had died at the
mission the previous day. I photographed
him leading this tragic procession, accompanied by off-key chanting of the mourners,
to the tiny churchyard behind the mission.

On this particular day he was burying five
people, two adults wrapped in old sacks and
three children each in a large brown paper
sack which had once brought food into
Kaabong.

I visited Sister Rosetta, another Italian,
who ran the hospital dispensary housed in a
couple of sheds. Her kindly face was pale
and drawn with the effort of trying to cope
with such a catastrophe. She lifted a baby
girl in her arms and said the child would be

A small child feeds from the shrivelled breast of its
mother

Father Liapetti conducts a funeral service for famine victims, Karamoja, 1980

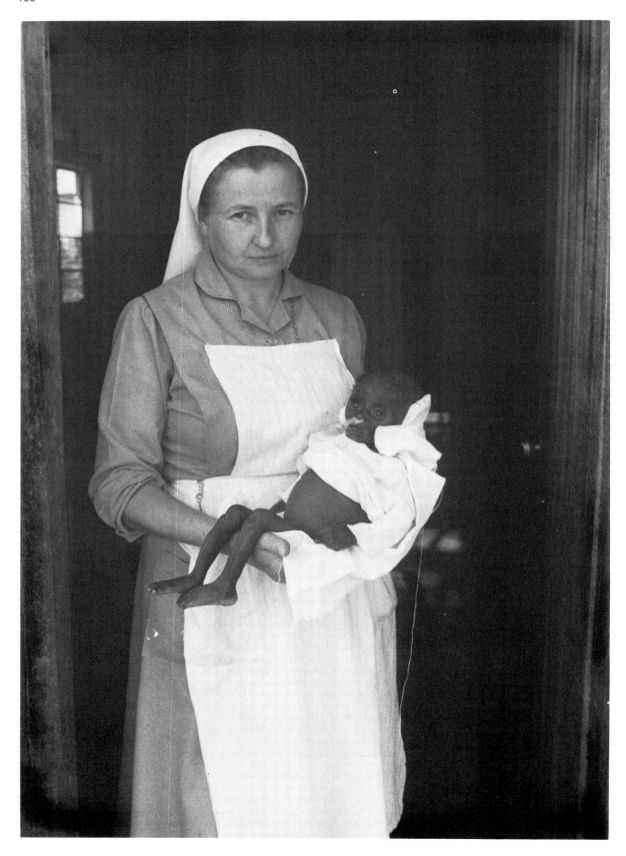

dead within an hour. Sister Rosetta showed me around the hospital where more children lay dying on iron bedsteads and I saw another small bundle covered by a blanket and waiting for Father Liapetti's funeral procession. She showed me the deep pit behind the hospital which was the only means of sanitation. I fought back an overwhelming need to be sick.

Before leaving I spoke to Sister Rosetta at length. She told me that she cried sometimes alone in her room and often felt like running away. 'But I can never leave these poor people,' she said.

Later I photographed her holding the body of the tiny girl whose death she had predicted less than an hour earlier.

Paul and I returned to Nairobi, then I flew back to London on a 747 which flew directly over the area where there was so much suffering. Sitting there in my comfortable seat, sipping a welcome gin and tonic, I tried to reason why such terrible things happen in a world so proud of its progress. Why, despite all efforts to get food into Karamoja, were children still dying every day? Survival for these people was so near yet so far away. It was incomprehensible to me.

I was disappointed by the small space which those pictures eventually made in the newspapers. In fact, I was angry. I felt they deserved more, and was reminded of the similar treatment given to the Vietnamese Boat People story.

Shortly after my return from Uganda I was taken ill with a bad bout of malaria. I

Sister Rosetta holds the body of a dead baby girl

was rushed to Guildford Hospital and was soon between crisp white sheets with doctors and nurses and the wonders of modern medicine to look after me. In shame, at the contrast between my predicament and that of those poor kids with nothing but the hot, dusty ground to lie down and die upon, I tried to dismiss the agony of the fever.

The fever eventually passed and while I was convalescing June received a telephone call from the *Irish Sunday Independent* newspaper in Dublin. They told her that my pictures and story of the Karamoja region had been used as part of a fund-raising appeal for the famine and my work had indirectly helped in raising a substantial amount of money which would be spent on getting more aid into Karamoja.

That, for me, is total job satisfaction.

I'm fifty years old now. I've been a photographer for more than 30 years and, looking back on my career, I realize how fortunate I was to choose a profession which has taken me practically everywhere there is to go. I have experienced a short period of history in the making. I've seen leaders come and leaders go and I've met kings and queens.

I have seen despair, famine and wars and I have cried more than once because of these things. But I've met some wonderful people, made lots of friends and laughed a lot, too. In short I've never regretted a single day of it. Today, I'm looking forward to my next assignment: 'Destination unknown.'